TI GREATEST SERMON EVER PREACHED

An investigation and personal reflection upon the Sermon on the Mount by Jesus c. 30AD, as recorded in the Gospel according to Matthew (Chaps. 5-7)

TIM HIGGINS

Acknowledgements

Many thanks to a few people here; to Keith Giles, who answered my desire for an endorsement from a published author as I venture out for the first time as a solo writer. To John Thompson and Jackie Pollock, who provided a modicum of feedback on my writing when I was testing the waters with my previous ideas, and to anyone who has made comments on my many blogs and vlogs that have been taken on board.

Not least to my long-suffering soulmate, Karen, who has been with me through every experience and trial of the past 34 years, and held me up when I was down, and rejoiced along with me when I was up.

To Laurann.
Be Blessed.

Love in Jesus,
Tim

Contents

Part 2: Be Humble

Part 3: The Heart Transformed

One of the most significant things about the Sermon on the Mount – and there are many – is just how upside down everything looks from our vantage point.

Jesus starts things off by listing for us the sorts of people who are "Blessed" in the Kingdom of God, and it looks nothing like the world we are born into. Where we live, the "Blessed" are driving Lamborghinis and dressing in designer clothes, they are not the poor, or the persecuted, or the peacemakers. In our world, those whom Jesus says are "Blessed" are at the bottom of the pyramid, getting crushed by those at the top who own all the wealth, have all the power and seemingly wield all the influence.

But once you start to follow Jesus – and this is most certainly the very point of the Sermon on the Mount – you start to realize something very profound: It's not the Kingdom of God that is upside down, it's our world that needs to be made right-side-up again.

See, what Jesus describes for us is the Kingdom of God, which is to say, the way God sees reality. It's the order of things that God intends, and has always intended, for us to follow. Our world has drifted so far off this intended course that we are now living in an upside down world where what should be up is down, and what should be right is all wrong.

In other words, we need to be reoriented to the Kingdom of God if we have any hope of becoming the sorts of people who reflect the glory, image and character of God as revealed for us in Jesus Christ.

So, what's the cure? Very simply, as Jesus puts it, the only answer is for us to obey him when he says to us, "Follow me."

When we begin to do this – to follow the way of Jesus – we start to learn how to re-think everything – or as Jesus said, to "Repent," (literally *Metanoia* meant to rethink or think differently). We start to become transformed into the image of Christ; slowly, almost imperceptibly, yet still inevitably changed by His Spirit into people who look, act, love, forgive and serve like Jesus did/does.

At the risk of sounding like an old man, It is very much like taking the red pill [as seen in the film *The Matrix*] and finding ourselves wide awake in a reality which is upside down and backwards from the world we have been born into. At first, we may reel with the vertigo of a world where the first are last, those who humble themselves are exalted, the greatest is the servant of all, and those who lose their lives find everlasting, eternal life, even though they die daily. But eventually we begin to get our bearings. We realize the beautiful truth: We are living in the Kingdom of God!

If you've made this step, let me say: Welcome to reality. Because this upside down world, we soon find, is NOT upside down, it is right side up. You see, we have lived so long, head over heels, immersed in an illusion of selfish fulfillment and a pursuit of more, more, more, that we recognize our need to detoxify our minds and hearts and flesh in order to function in God's Kingdom Reality.

Jesus announced this Kingdom, told us how to see it, how to walk in it and remain in it, and gave us the best news possible: We could enter and begin living in Reality anytime we wanted to. Right now. Today!

But, we also need to realize a few other important truths. First of all, that in the Kingdom of God there is just one King; God Himself. Now, the great news is that He is a good, loving, kind, and wildly, unpredictably, sometimes uncomfortably intimate, inclusive and wonderful king, and Father, and friend.

His Kingdom is a place where His perfect will is always done and those who rest in His will are refreshed and delighted and fulfilled and at peace and overjoyed. In His Kingdom, we are children once born into the poverty of excess wealth and unbridled selfishness who have now been adopted into a new Family of the unending wealth of generosity, knowing the true joy of always having enough to share and give away.

This is reality. Before God made this vast oasis called "Space and Time" there was no space or time. Everything was perfectly "Now" and Eternally present with Him. This is the only reality there has ever been. God's Kingdom was, and is, and is to come.

We also must recognize that our temporary stay in this unusual experiment called "Time and Space" will eventually expire and the temporary Kingdoms of this Earth will soon fade away. Make no mistake: The Kingdom of Pleasure will fall to the ground. The Kingdom of Greed will perish. The Kingdom of Exploitation and Oppression and Excess and Fashion and Wealth and Flesh – every earthly Kingdom – will eventually crumble and burn and disappear into oblivion. Only one Kingdom will remain and that is the Kingdom which was here "In The Beginning" – which has even now come, and which we can enter today.

What's more, one day soon, this everlasting Kingdom will break forever into this illusion we drift through for the moment, and overtake all we see and know.

Are you ready to enter this Kingdom? Are you ready to begin living under the awesome rule and reign of The King? There's just one thing, before you take that leap, before you swallow the red pill, that you should know, so that you can count the cost.

You see, those who enter the Kingdom can only step across the threshold if they pay the price. It's really nothing when you think about it, when you compare the amazing riches of God's Eternal Kingdom with the tokens and trinkets of our counterfeit reality. The price of admission, the way to step across, is to let go of this world.

So, just as you were born naked and weak and vulnerable and empty-handed into this world, so you can take nothing with you into God's Kingdom. It's called being "Born Again".

The things of this world are not truly treasures. When you die they will stay here anyway, and just as you can take nothing with you beyond the grave, you can take nothing with you when you step into God's Kingdom.

Jesus only asks for one thing- It's called "everything."

But what you gain, what you receive in exchange, is beyond anything you can dream of or hope for or imagine. The Kingdom of God, when you see it, when you really understand it, you will gladly rush out to sell all that you have, as quickly as possible, to step across the threshold into Heaven.

This is the moment where many people stop and turn back. Their grip on this world, or its grip on them, is so strong that they can never let go of their tiny, petty lives in this place in order to receive real life and treasure in God's Kingdom.

But, if we have really seen the Kingdom, if we really understand and believed that this Kingdom is real (in a way that nothing else can ever be *real*), then we will rush quickly to surrender all that we have and all that we are in order to receive the treasure that does not rust or face or disappoint.

*"For whoever wants to save his life will lose it,
but whoever loses his life for me will save
it." (Luke 9:24)*

*"The Kingdom of God is like treasure hidden in a
field. When a man found it, he hid it again, and
then in his joy went and sold all he had and
bought that field. Again, the Kingdom of heaven
is like a merchant looking for fine pearls. When
he found one of great value, he went away and
sold everything he had and bought it." (Matthew
13:44-46)*

So, you see, all God wants is all of you. All He asks is that
you trust Him and believe Him and surrender your meager
treasures and petty personal kingdoms in exchange for
His glorious, unending Kingdom.

God wants to be your God. He wants you to be one of His
People.

*"If anyone would come after me, he must deny
himself and take up his cross daily and follow me"
- Jesus (Luke 9:23)*

Simply put: There is no other way but the way of the
cross.

Jesus says it is very hard for a rich man to enter the
Kingdom of God:

*"It is easier for a camel to go through the eye of a
needle than it is for a rich man to enter the
Kingdom." Who then can be saved? His disciples
asked. "With man this is impossible," Jesus
replied, "But not with God; all things are possible
with God." (Mark 10: 23-27)*

So, the only question to ask is this: Will you let go? Will
you surrender it all? Will you seek first the Kingdom of
God and His righteousness? This is the only question we

need to answer in order to step across the threshold into the amazing reality of God's Kingdom.

Now, you can stay here, on this side of reality, where you are safe and miserable, in your tiny kingdom where your will is what matters. Or you can sell it all, exchange the handful of crumbling mud for real treasure which lasts forever.

Let me ask you: Is your kingdom so wonderful? Aren't you tired of wearing the crown? Haven't you suffered long enough under your own rule and reign?

There's no rush. Whenever you are ready to set fire to your kingdom, and surrender your lordship, and dance as the flames consume your empty way of living, He is ready to invite you to experience Reality, today.

This is the Good News: There is only One King, and He is good. He really wants what is best for you, and He can, above all, beyond any other, be Trusted. His Name is Faithful and True.

"I am the Way, the Truth and the Life and no one comes to the Father but by me" – Jesus (John 14)

For those of you who are ready to take this step, I can assure you, it's more than worth it. This book is designed to help you walk in this way of Jesus more easily and joyfully.

My friend Tim has done great work here to help you see the Kingdom more clearly. I know you'll be blessed as you dive in to these next few pages. But, when you're finished with the book, I hope you'll take the very necessary step of putting these things into practice. Because this is where the Kingdom is truly experienced – in our every day, waking lives.

Jesus is calling you, and me, and everyone on this planet, to make a very simple decision. The invitation begins here, with the way we respond to the invitation of Jesus: "Follow me."

I hope to see you on that road, my friend.

-**Keith Giles**, Program Director for Peace Catalyst International (Texas), and author of several books including, *Jesus Unbound: Liberating the Word of God from the Bible.*

Setting out my stall…

This is part of a larger book I had been attempting to write for some time; 'The Pursuit of Contentment'. I had been writing chapters on various topics. I stalled when writing about church when I realised I had to change church and learn a whole new way of viewing it, and the book ground to a halt for a few years as I went through this process. That issue will be the subject of a completely new book next for me.

Since I had believed I had dealt with some topics in their entirety, I decided to break up the book into smaller works to be published as ebooks. The first issue of 'contentment' I dealt with was the concept of sin, which for me has always been a dilemma; is it 'breaking commandments' or just 'acting selfishly'? Does it only apply to the 'big issues' like murder and adultery, or is every tiny infringement of a command like 'working on a Sunday' actually 'sinful'? Also, how do we decide who are the 'sin police' that we must listen to? As a follower of Jesus, I know that my whole life should be dedicated to 'following him' (makes sense!), so for me that is obeying his direct commands and seeking each day to be a better follower than I was yesterday. Do you not feel the same draw towards that kind of walk with him? A true pilgrimage on a spiritual plane? In all the years I spent trying to sort through these questions I had, I was consistently drawn back to **his** words. I realised that there was an awful lot of commands in the OT (Old Testament) law. Since we have a clear teaching from Jesus where he overstepped many of these rules and gave us different commands, then I can, as a Jesus Follower, a definitive Christian, focus on these and not worry about the ones that he dismissed in the same sermon. That was my 'simple' conclusion. The difficulty comes when we try to apply these teachings and live them out, because they go against every grain of natural thought in our heads and feeling in our hearts. I therefore decided that the best thing to do would be to pick apart that sermon and analyse it for ourselves. The teachings in it are recorded in all the gospels, in slightly different settings and formats, but since I am convinced that Jesus taught these things to different crowds and different people multiple times (as any traveling preacher would do), I think the Sermon on the Mount as recorded in Matthew's gospel (chapters 5 to 7) is the most concise example we have of 'the teachings of Jesus'.

Since the chapter on sin in my book became focussed mainly on parts of the Sermon on the Mount, I decided I should expand on the whole sermon, seeing it as 'The Manifesto of the Kingdom of God' and effectively create a commentary on Matthew 5 to 7. This is where Jesus sets out his blueprint for us and how we should live, think and act. It is a very concise piece once you analyse it. Why wouldn't it be? Those who preach set out with a plan before they write or speak any words. At least they **should**! Jesus clearly had a plan to his sermon, and we shall discover it here as we analyse. Other things that Jesus said, and what others wrote in our NT (New Testament) will be looked at too.

In trying to sort through the huge mass of scripture that we are told we have to follow and obey, have you never felt that you want to reduce it all down to something simple? Some think that the Ten Commandments do that, but Jesus both simplified that **and** expanded on it. Wow! The simplification was to reduce the law down to just two things:

> *Jesus replied: "'Love the Lord your God with all your heart and with all your soul and with all your mind." This is the first and greatest commandment. And the second is like it: "Love your neighbour as yourself." All the Law and the Prophets hang on these two commandments.* (Matt. 22:37-40)

Burn that simplification into your mind and your heart, and the expansion is what we shall deal with in the rest of this book...

Contentment with sin?

I discovered Jesus at a Scripture Union camp at 14, coming from an atheist home that never sent me to church or Sunday school. At this camp, we were given mini-sermons, testimonies, and exercises like scripture memory. The first verse I memorised, before I even became the Jesus Follower that I am, was that wonderful promise of 1John 1:9: *If we confess our sins, he is faithful and just and will forgive us our sins and purify us from all unrighteousness.* - **our sins are forgiven!** However, a problem arises, since we could easily draw the conclusion that we can continue to sin in our lives and simply ask forgiveness, like the proverbial boy who went to the minister to confess: he told him he was tempted to steal a bicycle he saw lying unlocked, and then he prayed about it. "Did the temptation leave you?" the minister asked. "No," he replied, "but I just decided to ask for forgiveness after I stole it!"

3

Personally, I have never come across anyone who actually believes this, but they do exist. Many preachers who overemphasise the doctrine of grace can imply it, almost licensing a congregation to have no worries about wrongdoing! Paul addresses this in his great treatise on grace in Romans:

> *What shall we say, then? Shall we go on sinning, so that grace may increase? By no means! We are those who have died to sin; how can we live in it any longer?* (Rom. 6:1-2)

Surely this is intuitive and natural to us? How could we, as followers of our perfect saviour, entertain the thought that sin doesn't matter? I use the word 'overemphasise' with caution, since for me, grace itself **cannot** be overemphasised: it is the linchpin of the Christian faith, and without it, **all** that we believe and live by in the gospel of Jesus Christ is folly! What **becomes** overemphasised is a notion that somehow, since God's grace is fully shown when he forgives sin unequivocally, then the more that we sin, the more his grace is shown to others - this is a nonsense that Paul dismisses in the one fell swoop I just quoted above.

We who say we follow Jesus seek a righteous life, a path that turns the opposite way of self and of following the ways of the world around us. We need to make a qualification at this point, because there are two things that get conflated (combined into the same thing); justification and sanctification. I'll avoid any detailed theological treatise on these things since there are many opinions and expounding on them in many books already, but basically;

> *justification* - the salvation from the consequences of our sins, achieved on Calvary,
> *sanctification* - the process we undergo in order to remove the present effects of sin in our bodies and lives, and by which we seek to attain a less sinful nature, each and every day on Earth.

Thinking that justification is equivalent to sanctification is what leads to what Dietrich Bonhoeffer called 'cheap grace'; the idea that you can have salvation without repentance, when Jesus clearly commanded his followers to obey him:

> *If you love me, keep my commands.* (John 14:15)
> *You are my friends if you do what I command.* (John 15:14)

Everything in me that has studied and debated theology for most of my life reacts to such words with a desire to express justification as 'finding Jesus' and sanctification as 'following Jesus'. You might ask is it that simple, and my answer is yes! We shall see what Jesus says about those who don't 'keep his commands' later... no, it's **not** 'salvation by works'!

It is by knowing exactly what he commanded that we are able to arrive at the hub of what we should do, and his expansion on these 'legal requirements' in his sermon then lead us to the very basics of 'Christian living' untainted by anything else which may have been added or embellished over 2000 years of church history. In all the years I have followed him, I have sought to get right back to these basics, to become like that kernel of followers who **knew** him and listened to his words, and went out to live it out as best they could. If I could throw off everything else that we, the church, have added to it, would that not be a wonderful place to be?

The ongoing sanctification that we are in the process of is what we need to address: **how** can we be content when we are well aware of the imperfection (which we can label 'sin') that still remains in us? How can we have reassurance that it actually does **not** matter in regards to our justification? The main threat that could undermine our faith in our own justification (how we **know** we have been 'born again') comes from that same first letter of John I memorised a verse from all those years ago:

> *No one who lives in him keeps on sinning. No one who continues to sin has either seen him or known him. Dear children, do not let anyone lead you astray. The one who does what is right is righteous, just as he is righteous. The one who does what is sinful is of the devil, because the devil has been sinning from the beginning.* (1John 3:6-8)

This was always a real wrestle for me! I **know** that I do continue to sin. I make mistakes daily, and the mistakes I make mean more to me than for those who do not have Jesus' standard to follow! If I am 'continuing to sin' then does John tell me that I have not 'known him'? How do I get through this? I cannot be content to continue a 'life of sin' but can I be content to know that occasional 'slips' are acceptable? Are they acceptable? Such doubts can plague our thoughts, and they must be dispelled in order for grace to be established. I treat such negative thoughts about my position with Jesus as the work of The Accuser (we will analyse this name later); I don't need to worry because the work is **his**, not mine. My desire to obey him is the response to his infinite love and is not works where I try to achieve what grace cannot, since grace achieves all for me, and this desire to obey him is only the proof that his Spirit is working within me and guiding me to do that.

Part of the problem in looking at 'sin' is having to define what **is**, and what isn't sin. For example, many modern believers decry smoking as 'sinful' because they read *Do you not know that your bodies are temples of the Holy Spirit* (1Cor. 6:19) as a truly corporeal thing and so smoking 'harms' this temple. Yet very few of them would afford the same definition to gluttony, despite a doctor telling them they're harming themselves **and** the fact that gluttony is mentioned in scripture while smoking is not - just to clarify this: scripture was written long before anyone outside the Americas knew about tobacco! If an obese person tells someone not to smoke, a little cringe occurs in me somewhere. Jesus' sermon will outlay some really good principles that we shall discover.

In many things that require some thought or debate, I find human nature taking either one extreme view or the other. The realisation that the message of the gospel of grace is really 'too good to be true' can lead to the stance that it **is** just so good, and thus the cheap grace is adopted, with the carefree attitude of 'sure we **are** forgiven, past, present and future, so why continue to worry? It was done on Calvary, finished, so don't sweat it!' This has basic flaws in it. I cannot find a blanket term for such preachers who grant licence too much.they may appear to be relatively new in terms of their coverage across accepted media and come from different sources, but we have seen that Paul addressed this in Romans 6, so it's not really new: there is *nothing new under the sun* as the Teacher wrote so long ago (Ecc. 1:9). With no better definition, I shall denote them as 'licensers'.

However, the other reaction, that somehow finds it to **not** be true, since it cannot accept that his grace is truly what it says on the tin, and that acceptance of his forgiveness could **not** be all that is required, can easily fall into legalism, which is usually the belief that we are still required to keep the whole law of the OT in order to assure ourselves of our salvation. It can also be a variation on that with a church or denomination outlining a number of 'behaviours' that it deems to be vital to follow. Take the example of the Roman Catholic definition of 'mortal sin' over 'venial sin' - many who have, since the Reformation, dismissed such doctrine, have fallen into the same trap of naming their own definitions of mortal sin even if they never used that label. This path has basic flaws in it (in fact, **major** flaws!), which Paul addresses with overwhelming arguments in his letters. When I read Paul's words, I am struck that he **does** certainly decry sin, but that it is **legalists** that he reserves his greatest condemnation for. In his letter to the Galatians, he gets really irate and heated about legalists who have '*bewitched*' them (3:1)! Maybe you have heard the phrase 'scandalous grace' (there is certainly at least one song entitled such or 'scandal of grace')? There is a reason for it. In 1Cor. 1:23, Paul states *but we preach Christ crucified: a*

stumbling block to Jews and foolishness to Gentiles...;
here, and in a few other verses, the word translated as
'stumbling block' is *skandalon*, from which we directly get
'scandal'. The message of Christ crucified, and of God's
grace that is imparted to us by that glorious death, **is** a
stumbling block. We have a problem in many modern
churches that state that they see it as a stumbling block to
those outside the church who 'do not wish to follow
religion'. The problem is it's actually the very **opposite**! In
the context, note that Paul was referring **to the Jews** who
were trying to hold onto their law, and Paul well knew,
having been one himself, that it causes offence to their ears;
the idea that all their lawkeeping and striving after God's
favour (their religion) can be done away with in one stroke,
and that acceptance of this one act, granted for all time,
renders anything else done in pursuit of forgiveness of sins
actually both futile **and** obsolete. **That** is scandalous, let us
be honest, to we who naturally think that people who make
no effort to live rightly and in peace and harmony with
others in society deserve any reward. It was also scandalous
to Mohammad who heard it and decided that it was just **not**
fair that those who never made an effort to live religiously
should be granted salvation as easily as anyone else, and so
he formed his own new religion, telling followers that they
could not expect God to just graciously forgive them unless
they made some effort for him. **If** you hear any preacher try
to say anything akin to this, politely tell them they may just
as well convert to Islam! **Yes!** The message of grace that is
the core of the Christian gospel (the 'good news') is most
definitely scandalous! I must confess that despite John
making it clear that this does not include the one who 'goes
on sinning', I cannot help but react against statements like
"you cannot live wrong and die right!" (though I appreciate

9

the 'anti-licenser' feeling behind it) since it flies in the face of that scandalous grace. Technically, **any** 'sinner' can find Jesus in their dying minutes. We often hear it proclaimed: "our sins are forgiven; past, present **and** future!" - is this true? Yes, the writer to the Hebrews stated that Jesus *offered for all time one sacrifice for sins* (10:12, emphasis mine), and it can **only** be that way - let us propose that we take 1John 1:9 absolutely literally, in that all sins must be confessed before they can be forgiven, then we can easily fall into a trap of paranoia that believes that were we to be taken from this life with a committed sin not confessed to God, we should not avail of forgiveness. There are people with obsessive personalities that would dwell on this every waking second, thinking that the smallest sin committed and not confessed before a car smashed into them would land them in hell! This is just **ludicrous**! Grace has done it all, it is all done, **was** done, already, as Christ shouted out on the cross *it is finished!* (John 19:30). Can you see how legalism utterly **undermines** the gospel?

And so I find myself quite emphatically in the camp against legalism, **but** I still have deep disdain for the licensers, and more importantly, I have to contend with the apostle John, and his annoying finger-wagging at those who 'go on sinning' - just how do I get out of this quagmire? Do you not have this same struggle? If not, I would love to ask you why. Or better still, how?

I recall the time I climbed Slieve League in Donegal; there is a part called 'One Man's Pass' since it is such a narrow path of rock that two could not walk together, with very steep drops on both sides - my friend said "there's nothing on one side, and even less on the other!" In our theology,

we must strive to find some middle ground where we avoid
the pitfall of legalism but do not stray over the other side of
the precipice into licence to sin. It, too, is a narrow path that
may be difficult to remain on, and I wonder often how
many ways we can allegorise the teaching Jesus gave about
the broad and narrow paths (Matt. 7:13-14 - we shall
examine that near the end). However, strive to follow on it
we **must** - Jesus made it clear that this 'following him'
business would be neither easy (Matt. 16:24), nor cheap
(Luke 9:57-62; 14:25-33). We must never be content to
reside in either of those depths that lie below our high
calling to follow Jesus. That calling that Jesus lays out for
us can be summed up as 'the Law of Christ' that Paul refers
to in Galatians 6:2 - *Carry each other's burdens, and in this
way you will fulfil the law of Christ.* There has been much
wrestling with what Paul means, since Galatians is his great
treatise **against** legalism, so why refer again to 'law'?
Instead of getting bogged down in difficult essays about
covenant theology and debates on doctrine, let us simply
look at what Jesus taught his own followers clearly and
simply, as they listened to his words. We shall see that
Jesus had a standard all his own, outside and above 'the
law'! However, before we look at his own distinct standard,
let us examine a simple but very important question I posed
earlier:

Original sin?

How do we define sin? There are many simple answers
given that somehow don't satisfy since they all have glaring
holes in them. For instance, we can say that sin is
'disobeying God' but then we need to define what exactly it
is that God has commanded or is commanding us now to

do, and that varies quite a lot - just look at all the theological interpretations that we have across different churches over 'lesser' doctrines, which is nothing new: the rabbinical tradition with all the differing interpretations of the nuances of the law did it thousands of years ago. We may also try to simplify it to 'doing harm to others' but as we shall see, Jesus commanded many things that are internal to us and have no physical action or consequences for others. One of the better ways of looking at what sin is, is to label it as 'selfishness' - the actions of the selfish person quite often **do** harm others, and while I believe that much of my conclusions here will fit in with that, it again is not a whole or complete answer. Can we come to a clear definition? Maybe it would help to go back to the beginning? I have often heard that the 'original sin' of Eden, by Adam and Eve, was 'pride' but I have never felt wholly comfortable with that, and here's why… there are certainly things that it is good to take pride in. I can feel proud of my children when they achieve a goal or pass an exam. Surely I am even entitled to take some pride in my own achievements? Otherwise I would not have a photo of myself holding my Master's degree in my Master's coloured robes! So 'pride' can have positive and negative connotations. This is partly due to historical linguistics, since many words in modern bible translations that we read as 'pride' are rendered 'glorify' or 'magnify' in the KJV - used in a verbal sense of 'magnify mine office' or 'give you occasion to glory in…' The KJV would seem to reserve 'pride' for the negative sense of boasting or arrogance, yet the positive coinages are still from original words that carry both the negative and positive, so we end up still in some uncertainty about just how bad pride really is. Please note that the very term 'original sin' came originally from

Augustine (354-430 AD) and not before then. Since his theology was the basis for much of Roman Catholicism, and also a lot of the continuation of concepts that the Reformation never shook off, we have to go right back to Eden to look at what 'the fall' was about, and bypass Augustine and all the other theologians. I truly believe we, as individual followers of Jesus, can do this, and **should**, as Jesus taught us:

> *Beware the teachers of the law.* (Luke 20:46)
> *Be on your guard against the yeast of the Pharisees and the Sadducees.* (Matt. 16:6)

One of the Greek words used in discussions about 'pride' is 'huperecho' which I could transliterate as 'hyper-ego' and this certainly is the underlying sense of the negative usage - an exaggerated sense of oneself, an inflated ego. Just as Paul warns all his readers, *do not think of yourself more highly than you ought* (Rom. 12:3), we are not to think of ourselves incorrectly. However, there is nothing wrong with being honest, surely? I have a pet hate: false humility. When I tell someone that they are good at something or that I appreciate the great job they did for me, I hate it when they become self-deprecating and say things like "oh no, I'm not that good" or "it's a terrible job, really" when they truly know that they **did** do well. This makes me look supercilious or haughty when I take such praise and just say things like "thank you" or "yeah, I was pleased with the job myself!" I'm just being honest, so hopefully when I do reject praise, it's because I truly think I don't deserve it, and not said out of a social norm that I'm meant to put myself down. Some of us have low enough self-esteem that a bit of straightforward analysis is a good thing!

So... is pride the original sin that man committed? Noting the exclusively negative usage in the KJV, I could embark on an examination of the diachronic language change ('changes in how we use words over time' to the layman) and suggest that we have seen a change in English in the usage of 'pride' which does not tally exactly with what a Jacobean reader in the 17th century understood it to mean: there are many examples of such words in the KJV being wholly different now e.g. charity, so I truly feel we must leave that version, wonderful though it **was** in its day, **to** its day, and respect its place in history (of both theology and the English language). Language change is as inevitable as the tide, so it is up to our bible translations to reflect that, not for us to try to make people understand an archaic form of English! (I'll not enter into any examination of the bad translations in the KJV that led to a lot of bad theology - that's for another time/ place/ blog/vlog/ book!)

I can see the basis, taking just the negative meaning, that a deliberate disobedience of a direct command from God comes from an inflated ego that thinks they know better than God (pride), but I still have problems with the label; it **is** behind what happened in the garden, but what was it that Eve **did** when she ate the forbidden fruit, and then offered it to Adam? She must have tasted that it was 'good' to offer it to him. There were two trees in the middle of Eden; the tree of life, and the tree of 'the knowledge of good and evil' (Gen. 2:9) - the fruit of one (along with the fruit of any other tree planted there) was allowed (life), and of one forbidden (the knowledge of... can we not think of a better word or phrase than that long phrase?). One thing to note is in her temptation, the serpent said to her ...*when you eat*

14

from it your eyes will be opened, and you will be like God, knowing good and evil. (3:4) So we have confirmation that eating it **will** impart such knowledge. No, hold on… these are the words of the serpent, which most scholars accept as Lucifer (The Accuser) masquerading. Of the different names that he has, a popular one is 'The Father of Lies' which was actually coined (or first recorded as) by Jesus himself (John 8:44), so before we simply accept what we read as 'the word of God' we need to recognise these words come from a liar, and from the originator of them. Some may think this reading of scripture is obvious, but some make such simple mistakes. So we must be wary of accepting it from **that** source that this was exactly what the fruit would give them. However, we can glean from the rest of the passage that this was correct - in verse 6 we read that Eve saw that the fruit was *also desirable for gaining wisdom* and more tellingly, in verse 11, after they hid from God because they were naked, God asked them: *Who told you that you were naked? Have you eaten from the tree that I commanded you not to eat from?* They had a new knowledge, that they were naked, so wished to cover themselves up from embarrassment, yet up to then, they were innocent and had no notion of being embarrassed before anyone, as Paul writes to Titus (1:15): *To the pure, all things are pure.* Adam and Eve had come to know the difference between good and evil (or **think** they had), and this was meant to be the preserve of God alone. He owned the tree, but they ate the fruit, and in that we have a picture I wish to portray to you; Adam and Eve thought they could acquire the same power (or **ability**) of God, but in taking just the fruit, they had a taste of what it would be like to be able to judge, but **only** a taste. The tree was not theirs, so they had not gained the full knowledge, only part of it, and

15

it was this ability to discern good and evil **to an extent** that they gained, thinking they were capable of more. There's an old proverb (generally attributed to Alexander Pope): "A little knowledge is a dangerous thing." How apt! Even in their hiding, they **should** have known that God would not be offended at their nakedness - he made them naked! - but they **believed** that they should cover themselves, so they lacked the ability to fully know God's mind, which would be required to be able to judge **correctly**!

And there we have the word I was seeking; the easier way to label this tree: **judge**! Can we not rename it 'the tree of judgment'? In attempting to be **like** God, they only came part of the way, so the deception of Lucifer (which means the 'bringer of light'), the original chief of angels, most beautiful and leader of the heavenly chorus, who then tried to be like God himself, is **most** clever since it contains a truth; *you will be like God, knowing good and evil*, yet this is not the whole truth since the likeness is only a shadow of God's power. Such is the language of the smartest deceivers we encounter; not exactly lies, but not exactly the truth either.

So then, may we grant this 'beginning' of sin a new name? (I even have a disdain now for 'original sin' since this was the basis for a far-reaching doctrine of human unworthiness begun by Augustine). I'm looking for a word more in keeping with our 21st century language and understanding? For me, were I to write my own paraphrase (a personal rewording of the original Biblical language and not a direct translation e.g. J.B. Phillips, The Message) of Genesis, I would simply call it "the Tree of Judgment"!

Anyone who knows their Bible in any measure must recall the many verses about judging! There are certainly procedures laid down for church discipline and decisions that church leadership must make, which would be for another book, but those are for specific situations and not for the individual to do. Jesus makes it very clear just where he wants us to stand on this:

> *Do not judge, or you too will be judged. For in the same way you judge others, you will be judged, and with the measure you use, it will be measured to you.* (Matt. 7:1-2)

We shall address this whole passage in Part 3. Jesus even makes it clear who is the only one capable of judging, and he states that he is not the one to judge, but only the Father in heaven:

> *If anyone hears my words but does not keep them, I do not judge that person. For I did not come to judge the world, but to save the world. There is a judge for the one who rejects me and does not accept my words; the very words I have spoken will condemn them at the last day.* (John 12:47-48)

So if we add to this how he stated *No one is good, except God alone* (Luke 18:19) and then see here how he left all the judging to God the Father alone, can we not discern a clear example he set? If even he has chosen not to judge people, then how could any one of us dare to think that we could make such judgments? We know that he was perfect and without sin (1Pet. 1:9) yet he himself declined to judge others, with a caveat that were he to decide to do so, it would only be because the Father was with him:

> *You judge by human standards; I pass judgment on no one. But if I do judge, my decisions are true, because I am not alone. I stand with the Father, who sent me.* (John 8:15-16)

I've been learning a lot about judgment recently, and by viewing the original forbidden tree as 'judgment' so much more has become clear: We never had the tree, only the fruit, but we **all** think we own the **tree**. Yet that belongs to God alone, and we are warned not to judge, but we **are** told we can discern people by their fruit:

> *Watch out for false prophets. They come to you in sheep's clothing, but inwardly they are ferocious wolves. By their fruit you will recognise them.* (Matt. 7:15-16)

Jesus repeats the warnings given here about the fate of 'unfruitful trees' in John 15, when he likens us to branches on a vine, which is himself, saying that his Father, the gardener, *cuts off every branch in me that bears no fruit...* and provides an example to his disciples when he cursed a fig tree for being unfruitful (Matt. 21:18-19). What exactly **is** the fruit? *But the fruit of the Spirit is love, joy, peace, forbearance, kindness, goodness, faithfulness, gentleness and self-control. Against such things there is no law.* (Gal. 5:22-23) Praise God, once we recognise that we are likened to trees; good and bad trees, known by good or bad fruit, we can separate people from their own fruit. We look for signs of fruit as has been laid out for us in the above list, and this should allow us to recognise those whom Jesus described as 'false prophets' and 'ferocious wolves'. We only need to think of the opposites to this to discern 'bad' fruit - hatred, misery, conflict, impatience, unkindness, evil, infidelity, brutishness, indiscipline, etc. Therefore we need to discern good and bad fruit i.e. people's actions or attitudes (or a political or religious belief or dogma that bears bad fruit), but **not** the tree itself - the person and their motives. Leave that to God. **We are not to condemn trees, just taste the fruit.** Again, this will be looked at in more detail in Part 3.

This brings to mind a saying a former pastor of mine used to like repeating: "If your attitude is wrong, you're **all** wrong!" This was reinforced recently when I came across a blog that questioned a saying that they heard, which was something like "that preacher may be a bit rude and unlikeable, but his theology is correct!" This really sat with me as uneasily as it did with the blogger: if we are to discern 'false prophets' by their fruit, as Jesus has made clear to us, then how can we defend a doctrinally-perfect minister who doesn't appear to have much of that 'good fruit'? Too often, we evangelicals try to discern others by marking their beliefs off against a 'heresy checklist' when actually we have a much simpler way. Of course, if you wish to look at doctrine, then it must be 'biblically-sound' and correct, I make no argument there, except to ask just what doctrines we are to be wary of, and how many are **really** based upon scripture or Jesus' words and are not embellishments - it's a difficult quest once you embark on it. Difficulty may arise when you have a church leader who is all smiles and lovely and makes you feel really warm and loved, but is preaching falsehood, but if a 'great doctrinal preacher' does **not** display proper fruit, can we not be led to conclude that they may not 'practice what they preach'? Again, that's the fruit, not the person.

Jesus' standard

When a rich young man came to Jesus, he asked him about eternal life:

> *Just then a man came up to Jesus and asked, 'Teacher, what good thing must I do to get eternal life?'*
> *'Why do you ask me about what is good?' Jesus replied. 'There is only One who is good. If you want to enter life, keep the commandments.'*
> *'Which ones?' he enquired.*
> *Jesus replied, '"You shall not murder, you shall not commit adultery, you shall not steal, you shall not give false testimony, honour your father and mother," and "love your neighbour as yourself."'*
> *'All these I have kept,' the young man said. 'What do I still lack?'*
> *Jesus answered, 'If you want to be perfect, go, sell your possessions and give to the poor, and you will have treasure in heaven. Then come, follow me.'*
> *When the young man heard this, he went away sad, because he had great wealth.* (Matt. 19:16-22)

Now here was a man who was able to state that he had kept all the commandments, yet he was still troubled in his spirit that he needed to do more. Jesus made it clear to him that he was right, and demanded a higher standard, that he had to give up his wealth. Let us try to grasp what Jesus was

20

doing here. The priests, rabbis and Pharisees of Jesus' day would just be concerned with the law, entreating their audiences to follow it and keep it, nothing more. When they encountered dilemmas, like 'if my donkey or my sheep falls into a pit on the Sabbath, am I lawful if I retrieve it, or is that 'work'?': this led to many debates and differing schools within the rabbinical tradition, so sorting through the apparent 'mess' that one encounters if one wishes to be exact to scripture is nothing new. Though I do believe that some teachers were able to get an idea from their scriptures that there was something deeper; Paul had studied under Gamaliel, a renowned Pharisee and teacher, and his grasp of living by faith and not by law leads me to ponder that he had already realised the truth that Abraham had lived long before the law was written and had been justified by faith - *Abram believed the Lord, and he credited it to him as righteousness.* (Gen. 15:6): Paul quotes this in his letter to the Romans in his argument about justification by faith. In fact, the belief in God was already there when he was still called Abram, before God gave him the new name of Abraham (Gen. 17:5). The law, not being written until Moses came along, was completely irrelevant to the lives and the righteousness of **everyone** that lived before then!

Jesus proclaimed a truly new message for the people of that time, who had come to be known as 'a people of the book': to all intents, they idolised their scriptures, which is a recurring problem again today - nothing new under the sun! His 'Sermon on the Mount' as recorded in Matthew's gospel (chapters 5 to 7) is the most concise, and greatest sermon ever preached, by the Son of God, no less. This is his Kingdom 'manifesto' and it is this which I wish to refer

to in order to get to the nub of this issue, and the hub of our
walk after Jesus…

The Sermon

The three chapters as divided in Matthew's gospel are the neat representation of what I see as a three-part sermon.

Chapter 5 is part 1: My Kingdom, My Rules

Chapter 6 is part 2: Be Humble

Chapter 7 is part 3: The Heart Transformed

Part 1: My Kingdom, My Rules

The Beatitudes

Jesus opens his sermon with a whirlwind! We have become so used to hearing these sayings that they roll off our tongue like poetry, which we have heard in churches and in our education too often to realise the impact they had when first uttered. They certainly **are** poetic. Beautifully poetic, but it's their **meaning** that is the shocker. We get so used to the 'Blessed are…' lines that we forget how nonsensical they really sound in our ears. Were we to strip away our religious background, we would approach these sayings with a sense of 'what on Earth is this guy going on about?' Even those who have had no religious upbringing, like me, have become so used to hearing these verses that we have been numbed to them, and think of them as poetic utterances of a dreamlike faraway place, where they are magically true. Is this not how we think about them? That they refer to heaven, the 'kingdom yet to come', and only to be viewed when perfection has been restored, so they really mean nothing right now?

It's because we have a 'worldly' view of blessing; that we think blessing is receiving things like wealth, strength, confidence, high position, social standing, etc. To an audience of human beings very like us, Jesus starts talking about blessing, on his own terms, and he turns the 'natural' perception of blessing on its head, entirely! I personally prefer the NLT version since it explains in better language for us today:

> *God blesses those who are poor and realise their need for him,*
> *for the Kingdom of Heaven is theirs.*
>
> *God blesses those who mourn,*
> *for they will be comforted.*
>
> *God blesses those who are humble,*
> *for they will inherit the whole earth.*
>
> *God blesses those who hunger and thirst for justice,*
> *for they will be satisfied.*
>
> *God blesses those who are merciful,*
> *for they will be shown mercy.*
>
> *God blesses those whose hearts are pure,*
> *for they will see God.*
>
> *God blesses those who work for peace,*

for they will be called the children of God.

*God blesses those who are persecuted for doing
right,*
for the Kingdom of Heaven is theirs.

Surely, we recognise some of these descriptions? We know
how many of them are ridiculed and derided by those in
power, by established norms, and even by many church
hierarchies? In recalling the original words from the KJV
(meek, peacemakers, poor in spirit), I realised just how
much we could paraphrase these terms and use others, still
apt for the context. We could use descriptors like
'peacenik', 'justice warrior', 'wimp', 'dreamer'… even
'snowflake'? These are the people that are told they will
not achieve anything. The powerful tell the peacemaker
that they must accept that war is vital because they just
don't understand the machinations of power, and that the
earth belongs to the victor. Some churches tell those whose
hearts are simple and easily pleased that they will **not** see
God because they aren't pedantic enough about their
doctrine to really understand who's 'in' and who's not.
How many parents tell their children that a 'crybaby' won't
get anywhere in life (especially to the boys!), and they need
to understand that or they'll get walked over? Yet here is
Jesus offering power and possession to the humble,
satisfaction and the Kingdom of Heaven to the campaigner,
and comfort to those who are mourning after loss. It's not
even just an offer, it's a statement! Note that the NLT
renders the translation 'God blesses' - the more common
rendition of 'Blessed are' is also present tense. If you
believe that God is the one who blesses, then he **does** bless
those who are being described. It's not 'Blessed will they

be'! These people **are** the ones that God blesses. Take hold of that, and know that if you fit into any of these descriptors, you are blessed, right now. It sometimes may not feel like you are blessed, but that surely comes from a skewed view of the universe? If Jesus tells me that I **am** blessed for being like this, then I know and accept that God's blessing is upon me.

Do we truly believe these things that Jesus was telling us all? If so, then why would we lower ourselves to be like those who seek power, fame and wealth. They are **not** the ones who are blessed, and they deceive themselves. They are not mentioned in this Kingdom. A few translations try to reword these to mean they only apply personally and inwardly, but thankfully most translators disagree. Those 'who work for peace' (peacemakers) are not working to make their **own** hearts peaceful! We shall also be blessed when persecuted for believing these things inwardly… **NO!** Persecuted 'for **doing** right' [emphasis mine]. This is not the sort of persecution by other religions for simply holding an internal belief, but for trying to work out our following of Jesus by working for the things that Jesus desires us to do, we will be persecuted. This is the persecution that Jesus states is the one we shall be blessed in. The other kind of persecution is not mentioned here, and is not being addressed.

Jesus then offers more comfort to those who might choose to follow this path and face the ridicule they are going to get from the world (and any church that might not want genuine **followers** to work for these things - no?):

*God blesses you when people mock you and
persecute you and lie about you and say all sorts of
evil things against you because you are my
followers. Be happy about it! Be very glad! For a
great reward awaits you in heaven. And remember,
the ancient prophets were persecuted in the same
way.*

We need to recall what the ancient prophets said and did,
and be aware how they railed against the norms of their
society. They were very often challenging the established
priesthood and the political leaders over what they
perceived God was asking of them, not least of which was
what Jesus quoted to the Pharisees from Hosea (6:6): *But
go and learn what this means: I desire mercy, not sacrifice.*
(Matt. 9:13). If these prophets were persecuted and
ridiculed for challenging the religious patterns the people
had fallen into and only tried to make them see how God
sought merciful hearts instead, then Jesus was letting us
know we would face the same once we challenged current
religious norms, but that we should be happy about that,
and **very** glad that we were in the same company,
regardless of whatever anyone else thinks. There is a
reward for us in heaven, but we will also receive God's
blessing through this time.

Is it not possible to recognise how this opening of his
sermon would have been a shock to the people gathered to
listen? What brought them all out to this place to hear him?
We know of all the miracles performed as described in the
previous chapter, but we also know of the later testimony of
the Temple guards who were sent to arrest him and returned
to the Pharisees empty-handed: *'No one ever spoke the way*

this man does,' the guards replied. (John 7:46). If that was not the reason for some of the people to come and hear him, it would certainly be what they were thinking now!

Salty people

> *'You are the salt of the earth. But if the salt loses its saltiness, how can it be made salty again? It is no longer good for anything, except to be thrown out and trampled underfoot.*
> *'You are the light of the world. A town built on a hill cannot be hidden. Neither do people light a lamp and put it under a bowl. Instead they put it on its stand, and it gives light to everyone in the house. In the same way, let your light shine before others, that they may see your good deeds and glorify your Father in heaven.*

Another statement that we have become familiar with; we are most likely to not grasp the impact, because we usually have it read to us in the context of church meetings. To recognise the impact it was meant to have, we have to go back to that time, and then discover the relevance for today. The audience Jesus is addressing is the vast crowds of ordinary people who came to listen, and not just his twelve disciples. Other passages are delivered to them alone, some to only a few of them, and some to a wider group of followers, but this is a different ball game entirely, like a mass rally at a stadium in comparison to a small enclosed church building. In other words, these people are what we have come to call the **laity**. The general 'hoi polloi' that weren't in the priesthood, or belonged to the Levites, or administered anything within the Temple, or maybe even their local synagogue. These 'priestly' people would very likely have been **in** the gathered crowd, but would only have comprised a small minority. So Jesus is addressing them directly and telling them that they are the 'salt of the earth' and the 'light of the world'... what? Ordinary folk with no education or any role to play in the current religious institution of Judaism? This is indeed radical! We often talk about the amazing growth of the first century church and the great works they accomplished, but we fail to see that the majority of them were these uneducated ones. The only scripture they had was what we now call the OT, and those were written in Hebrew, a language that had died in common usage (Jews then were speaking Aramaic). There was a Greek translation of the scriptures called the Septuagint (or LXX) for the Greek-speaking population, but again, only on a number of expensive, hand-written copies. The printing press would not be available for another 1400+ years! Jesus was certainly breaking a mould by telling the people that **they** would be salt and light to the whole world! We know that he said that **he** was the light of the world (John 8:12) too, so can we not grasp hold of his truth to us that he and the Father will come to us and 'make their home' with us (John 14:23)? If they are with us, we **are** the bringers of that shining light and the providers of the preserving salt. [If you wonder, as I did, how salt could 'lose its saltiness', consider that most salt then was not the clean white powder we all have in our kitchens, but was rock salt, a kind of gravel that had salt within it that would be leached out by contact in order, mainly, to preserve meat and fish in a time before refrigeration and vacuum packaging. When that rock salt no longer had any salt in it to dissolve out, it was just gravel and only fit to be used to fill holes in a path].

Very truly I tell you, whoever believes in me will do the works I have been doing, and they will do even greater things than these, because I am going to the Father. (John 14:12)

If every one of us who says we love Jesus and desire to follow him take hold of this in the here and now, what could be achieved for the Kingdom of Heaven on 21st century Earth?

'but I say to you…'

A huge portion of the Sermon conforms to a pattern, as he spoke, with "*You have heard that it was said…. But I tell you….*" as he recalls the commandments given to ancient Israelites but goes ahead and offers an alternative view. Is he setting them aside? No! He is **adding** to them! Let us list them briefly and then deal with each in detail:

You have heard that it was said….
> *'You shall not murder, and anyone who murders will be subject to judgment.'*

But I tell you…
> *that anyone who is angry with a brother or sister will be subject to judgment….*

You have heard that it was said….
> *'You shall not commit adultery.'*

But I tell you…
> *that anyone who looks at a woman lustfully has already committed adultery with her in his heart….*

You have heard that it was said....
> *'Anyone who divorces his wife must give her a*
> *certificate of divorce.'*

But I tell you...
> *that anyone who divorces his wife, except for sexual*
> *immorality, makes her the victim of adultery, and*
> *anyone who marries a divorced woman commits*
> *adultery.*

You have heard that it was said....
> *'Do not break your oath, but fulfill to the Lord the*
> *vows you have made.'*

But I tell you...
> *do not swear an oath at all...*

You have heard that it was said....
> *'Eye for eye, and tooth for tooth.'*

But I tell you...
> *do not resist an evil person....*

You have heard that it was said....
> *'Love your neighbour and hate your enemy.'*

But I tell you...
> *love your enemies...*

If you have read this entire sermon, you should be aware of a problem. Well, I was always aware, reading it. Right before these 'commands' that he gives, Jesus states something that has become the favourite passage of the legalists:

> *Do not think that I have come to abolish the Law or*
> *the Prophets; I have not come to abolish them but to*

fulfil them. For truly I tell you, until heaven and earth disappear, not the smallest letter, not the least stroke of a pen, will by any means disappear from the Law until everything is accomplished. Therefore anyone who sets aside one of the least of these commands and teaches others accordingly will be called least in the kingdom of heaven, but whoever practices and teaches these commands will be called great in the kingdom of heaven.

The first verse here (17) is a classic case of one being taken out of context, since many legalists quote just one part: '*I have not come to abolish [the law]*' or even misquote it in this example, since it was not 'the law' that Jesus meant when he said 'them' - he was talking of the Law **and** the Prophets, and he went on to say that he came '*but to fulfil them.*' Such quotes out of context tend to lead to a belief that this passage would appear to state that we must keep the whole law laid down in the OT. However, **context is everything!** - right after he says this, Jesus himself **seems** to go against it! Take one example for quick illustration: 'eye for eye, tooth for tooth' is repeated three times in the Torah, with admonishments to 'show no pity' so why tell his followers to ignore this? The next verse (5:20), which intervenes right before the 'reworking' of certain commands, tends to be overlooked unfortunately, but it lays out where he is going:

For I tell you that unless your righteousness surpasses that of the Pharisees and the teachers of the law, you will certainly not enter the kingdom of heaven.

The key word here is *surpasses*. In effect, Jesus is saying "yes, in the Law you are **permitted** to take restitution from anyone who has wronged you, 'eye for eye, tooth for tooth' but I want you to forego that and **not** demand any such recompense."

Jesus is **clearly** commanding his followers to look at this 'righteousness' that the Pharisees have by keeping every stroke of their law and see it as still not good enough for citizens of his 'kingdom of heaven' - they are to keep to higher standards, that affect them inwardly so much more than just religious observance of decrees, just like he had stated to the rich young man who **had** kept the commandments. I want to impress upon you that **Jesus raises the bar!** In our high jump over our problems with personal sin, Jesus does not make it easier, as the licensers would wish us to believe, or at least not in the way they would like him to. No, he makes it altogether **more** difficult. However, I want to show you how he also makes it **simpler...** take heart! There **are** ways through this. Let us look at these six '*but I say to you...*' statements of Christ in order:

Murder

> You have heard that it was said 'You shall not murder, and anyone who murders will be subject to judgment.' But I tell you that anyone who is angry with a brother or sister will be subject to judgment. Again, anyone who says to a brother or sister, '"Raca," is answerable to the court. And anyone who says, 'You fool!' will be in danger of the fire of hell.

First, right after stating that we must **surpass** lawkeeping righteousness, he delivers two bombs! On murder and adultery! Two serious issues that usually brought the penalty of death for transgressors. He addresses murder and then starts talking about anger and name calling! "What?" I'm sure the crowd were murmuring, "Does he really mean that me being angry with someone and insulting them is equivalent to murder?" There were **bound** to be listeners who laughed at him and switched off then; their self-righteousness allowing them to say "I'm no murderer!' However, those who understood who this teacher was, or at least what truth he spoke, would **still** have been shocked by this claim. How can murder be equated with calling someone 'Raca'? This was an Aramaic term of contempt that meant 'worthless' so probably equates with 'scum' in English, but 'fool' can also land us within throwing distance of 'the fire of hell', according to our Lord Jesus!! (This is actually a reference to 'Gehenna' but I shall not delve into that topic since it would create another book and there are plenty already written). My Ulster-Scots word of choice in this instance is 'eejit' (now officially in the OED and allowable on 'Countdown') and I confess I use it fairly often. So should I be condemned?

I look back on the years we had raising our son and daughter, and try to recall if I ever broke my own rule, and utter such insults in anger at them. We agreed that we would **never** call them 'stupid' or 'lazy' or call them a bad boy or girl, but instead admonish them not to **be** stupid, or not to **act** lazy, and try to reinforce that they in fact were **not** these things so we expected better from them, whenever they should transgress. Surely loving parents should seek ways to uplift their children and not bring them down? Though not by allowing bad behaviour, but disapproving of it while still loving the child. I wondered then if this is what Jesus meant; that we should love all people in the same way, and while we may have occasion to challenge unwanted actions or attitudes in others, we should not go so far as to slap negative labels on people (recall the tree and the fruit?). Such things bring judgment upon us, just as judgement would be given for murder under the law, so our lord truly is equating them. Everything in our limited human understanding rejects this, surely? I have never murdered anyone, but I've been angry with people on a fair number of…. well, it's just uncountable! And calling people eejits? I suppose **my** worst time for that is when I'm driving, since there are people who just should never have been given a driving licence! On most journeys I'll come across at least one! This could not be the same thing as murder, **surely**?

Right away, we come to a distinction, and it is one between what we constitute as law for living together in a society, and what God counts as righteousness. Many use the expression 'right living' but I shirk from that since for me it carries so many connotations of 'self-righteousness' and is just an alternative form of lawkeeping and legalism that states "I live by such and such a standard" and reeks to me of Pharisaism. It was such attitudes that Jesus encountered in the religious elite of his day that he condemned most vehemently, and I would wish that Christians would see it for what it is; another way of vaunting your own righteousness as 'better' than that of others, which may not be the **intention** of such 'standard' keeping but that is certainly what comes across to outsiders, too often. I know

35

that I had a clear picture in my mind, as a young atheist of 14, of the stereotypical churchgoer, but no clear picture of a Christian, except that they should just be nice people. Shouldn't they? No, I mean 'Shouldn't **we**?' This must make us conclude that no amount of law keeping will impress anyone, at the end of the day. Our 'higher standard' must be something else, something greater than what **any** person of **any** religious persuasion can do. This distinction needs to be highlighted; law is given for the administration of a code of living for all people to abide by, or face consequences. This we call **justice**. Righteousness that God our Father calls us to is **not** lawkeeping. We have already encountered Abram, who lived long before Moses wrote the law down for the Israelites, but who, as an individual, was **counted** righteous by his faith in God. So when **we** think of ourselves as righteous because of any 'standard' we might choose to keep, we must remember how the prophet Isaiah summed that up: *All of us have become like one who is unclean, and all our righteous acts are like filthy rags* (64:6). I like how The Message renders it: *Our best efforts are grease-stained rags*. No matter how hard we may try, we cannot attain to God's standard, *for all have sinned and fall short of the glory of God* (Rom. 3:23). Note that I have already dismissed the far-reaching doctrine of 'original sin' because it includes attitudes that go beyond what Jesus is actually saying to us. I have always viewed grace as a universally empowering sacrament from Christ for all our lives, and never liked how it was malformed into a means of 'selection' of one person over another. While we have difficulty meeting this perfection that Jesus is laying out for us, grace is extended to us by him at the same time. Recall that even Jesus himself showed deference to this; in Luke's account of the rich young man, the young man addressed

Jesus as '*Good teacher*' and Jesus replied *Why do you call me good? No one is good - except God alone.* (18:19). Maintaining the attitude of humility with regards to his own 'goodness' (as we ascribe it to him), he shows that God's idea of 'good' is certainly higher than ours. With **this** frame of mind, and this view of the universe, Jesus' claim that we are sinning when we get angry with someone or insult them becomes a lot clearer. How, then, can we ever hope to maintain this standard higher than the law? One way many have managed this is to reinterpret it! I have listened to people who pride themselves as 'Biblical literalists' and who would accept **no** other interpretation of the creation except that it was six complete days and no more, who then approach these difficult words of our Lord's sermon with an attitude of "he clearly didn't mean as much as we think he meant" and go on to offer interpretations more 'acceptable' to our worldview. Why? If you're asking me, we all have a worldview that is shaped by many things around us, and we all like it, for it's what we have grown with over a long time, maybe even all of our lives, and we know many others within our circle, or our culture, who feel the same and believe the same. So, for instance, if we harbour deep feelings of resentment toward another nation, class, religion or ethnic group, for whatever reason, these instructions to not get angry with anyone and to love our enemies do not sit well with us. They prick us like cactus spines and we just don't like hearing them, and so we either do a juggling act with the words (which we apparently are not **allowed** to do with more 'fundamental' passages like Genesis 1!) or we cover our ears like one of the three monkeys! In over 30 years of listening to sermons, I cannot recall even one from a pulpit on these sayings of Jesus! That may be the fading memory of my middle-age, but I believe I would remember such a sermon, since they clearly are so rare. Must be things that preachers either just don't wish to tackle or that they think nobody wants to hear, although Jesus knew full well that his audience would not wish to hear them. I truly fear that many would try to introduce some caveats or 'get-out' clauses as if such anger and a natural desire for justice or recompense from an enemy somehow qualify as exempt from this clear, concise command: such interpretation cannot be good, for it opens the same door that Satan opened with Eve i.e. "**has** *God said...?*" - if Jesus said it, he meant it! While I am one to acknowledge there are many parts of our scripture that we can look at with fresher eyes of reinterpretation once we see that we may have read it incorrectly and been led more by tradition or our own cultural glasses, I believe these clear commands of Jesus are most definitely **not** up for renegotiation. Jesus then seems to go off on a tangent from this:

> *'Therefore, if you are offering your gift at the altar and there remember that your brother or sister has something against you, leave your gift there in front of the altar. First go and be reconciled to them; then come and offer your gift.*
> *Settle matters quickly with your adversary who is taking you to court. Do it while you are still together on the way, or your adversary may hand you over to the judge, and the judge may hand you over to the officer, and you may be thrown into prison. Truly I tell you, you will not get out until you have paid the last penny.'*

However, this does tie in with his teaching on anger; firstly, remaining angry with a brother/ sister is not acceptable to God, as he has just outlined, so it must be applied practically. We cannot come to perform some act of religion if this exists in our heart. The equivalent of making an offering in churches today has often been seen as partaking of communion. It could also be when we make an offering of money into the basket (more apt analogy?). Whatever it is that we attempt to do for God, such activity must be put on hold until existing anger is assuaged. Note how Jesus places the emphasis on the other party having something against **us**! Such a situation may well on most occasions have created anger within both parties, but even if you yourself have no anger towards them, you are commanded to reconcile with them in order for **their** anger to be dealt with. We can tell Cain that we most certainly **are** our brother's keeper! We shall revisit how important mastering anger is when we come to 'an eye for an eye'.

Secondly, there may well be consequences of such anger and malice. Jesus exhorts us to settle disputes with people before our own pride and arrogance may land us in a legal mess. That's simply in addition to the benefit of living outside the worldly view of winners and losers, and the desire to always be right, or be seen to be right. If we have Christ within us, who cares if others think less of you or that you're wrong? As Paul reiterates to the Romans:

> *If it is possible, as far as it depends on you, live at peace with everyone.* (Romans 12:18)

Or as I saw in a great meme recently; nobody ever choked to death from swallowing their pride! I'm sure that you have experienced something similar to what I've gone through, or are even going through right now. As I was in the process of researching and writing this book, I found myself in a dark place, with a person close to me, whom I will admit at one point, I wished to beat to a jammy pulp!! Overcoming those feelings of anger was a struggle, but just as I arrived there, someone else even closer, so unexpectedly, turned against me. I was more able to avoid getting too angry with them, because I believe I had been able to apply these kingdom principles gleaned from the first example (and previous incidents I had experienced with fellow human beings). The application of the principle is easier the next time, and each subsequent experience, which then should lead to mastery. Mastering our anger is surely exactly what Jesus wants for us, from his previous warning about that emotion. I now feel that I would be unaffected by someone coming at me to attack me, or at least much less affected.

What **does** affect me is when there is realisation on my part that I **did** manage to fall short of this standard, while still knowing just how difficult it is! I wrote a whole paragraph of what I went through in the former experience, but I just deleted it all because it's no longer of any consequence to me. Those feelings that I had, which really welled up in me to want to do something physically (really!), are long gone. Praise God.

It is **only** the Holy Spirit within me that stopped me from fulfilling those visions of blood and joy that infested my thoughts. My temperament is a quiet and thoughtful one, and in my whole life I have seldom been given to violence: I could count those occasions on one hand, no doubt. I have a vivid recollection of a fallout with some friends when I was still primary school age; they took me into the garage of one of their houses to 'sort me out' but after that my memory is blank until I recall myself opening the door of the garage and walking out to a crowd of bemused kids who had heard the noise, with the three of them lying on the ground moaning. I have no clear idea just what I did but it was effective. I have always been aware of the potential within me to unleash such wrath, and so I have maybe shied from it through fear of some latent power that I may not control; are stories like 'Dr. Jekyll and Mr. Hyde' and characters like 'The Incredible Hulk' not just yarns about that which is within each of us; the monster? Throughout practically all my school years I suffered bullying in some small form, but I never once retaliated! I could say it is just not in my nature, but that incident in the garage would suggest otherwise. I believe that any of us, pushed far enough, could find the potential for wrathful vengeance on someone. I imagine that I would exact such strength on anyone to defend my children if they were attacked, and I am thankful that I never faced that terrible scenario.

However, I do know that I still possess the quality of a volcano - I can lie dormant for a very long time and not get annoyed, but when I have had enough of someone, I have been known to unleash verbally in a cataclysmic explosion that has left people standing with jaws agape. It hadn't happened for some time, so I tricked myself into believing it had been mastered, having mellowed in my recent years, but then I was pushed over the edge again about two years ago, with someone I never thought would 'trigger' me. I must continue to be vigilant to such feelings. In all that we have been going over with these commands, we must know that some things committed within our heads are as sinful to God as the corresponding actions: is this the same with violence? Since I am able to be aware of these thoughts, I can report that my spirituality was affected, and badly! Prayer was more difficult, even reading scripture to find what I needed to write this became a chore. So the effect of such anger makes me less likely to 'rise above it' spiritually and it becomes a downward spiral staircase.

Yet when I know I am being more spiritually-minded, those things are more natural. Indeed, such anger, even though internal, is negative upon me and on my efforts to follow Jesus. In order to be effective for Jesus and to be a 'good ambassador' for The Kingdom of God (as we are often told to be!), I must strive to put away all such violence from me and pray "Yes, Lord, even violent thoughts, wrath, anger can be damaging to the nature of my spirit that I need to communicate with you, and with others in whatever way I may. Help me to overcome it." So ask yourself: How often have you been angry at something or someone, and have snapped or shouted at another poor innocent who strayed too close to the grumpy bear you had become? I've lost count! While I think that patience is a strength of mine, it has a limit, and once that limit is reached, people need to run from the volcano.

So is anger then a sin? Not in itself, since we can get angry at injustice, inflicted suffering, poverty, unchecked disease among the poor, uncaring governments, false teaching from pulpits that undermines the gospel, etc. without falling into sin. Paul warned the Ephesians (4:26-27): *"In your anger do not sin": Do not let the sun go down while you are still angry, and do not give the devil a foothold.* Paul quotes "In your anger do not sin" from Psalm 4:4 from the LXX, but he is clearly warning of the inherent danger one faces when anger is engaged: letting it fester and grow "gives the devil a foothold" - I used to go rockclimbing in my younger days, and a foothold is far more advantageous and stronger than a handhold. Getting one foot up into a higher position in a good foothold grants the climber the best way of climbing higher, so we are not to let anger offer such a foothold to the Accuser so he may climb upon us and weigh us down. Paul knew that anger has this trait that can be used as a tool in the wrong way, so we need to be careful just how we handle it. How then can we be content with anger? When do we engage it and use it, and when do we stop ourselves from getting... **too** angry?

Anger

Looking at scripture, we may notice there are different words such as anger, wrath, rage, fits of rage, etc. depending on which version you use. We must look at 'wrath' since it stands out in the 21st century as a word that has fallen out of common usage, to the point that it is almost always associated with 'the wrath of God'; I have taken time to read quite a lot on this concept and how the word is translated from various words in Hebrew and Greek, and how different versions approach it. It is certainly a very interesting study to undertake, to see how it has been handled through different eras by different thinkers, but boiling it down to a practical application here has not been easy! There is much that I could say about the implications for theology with wrath and God, but I must leave that for blogging or maybe another book. As ever, there are plenty of books on the topic.

There are a number of Hebrew words used in the OT which correspond to wrath in the KJV, and just two Greek words in the NT. For our purposes here, without going into a great treatise on the variances in the languages, we should focus on the two NT words, *orgē*, and *thumos*. These two words are very similar in meaning, both coming from roots that originate from 'nostrils' or 'smoking/ fuming' with parallels in the Hebrew words, so they both relate to the metaphor of 'breathing fire' and 'fuming with anger' [a metaphor is a figure of speech that applies like a picture to something not literally appearing like it]. The NIV is more faithful to translate *orgē* in one way and *thumos* in another, whereas the KJV uses them a bit interchangeably. There is a consensus that *orgē* relates to the **actions** caused by anger, while *thumos* describes the **emotion** that wells up inside the angry person, though this still causes a certain amount of confusion since it doesn't seem to correspond to each instance. This is a time to repeat a great maxim I used earlier that we shall revisit many times: **context is everything!** If a particular verse doesn't seem to make sense or seem to contradict something else in scripture, placing it in its context i.e. reading the **whole** passage, or even the whole **book** can explain it. Usually! There certainly would be a case for arguing that such **actions** caused by anger are in a sense, rational.

What I'm taking from this study is that the **emotion** of anger that wells up within us is the one that can be irrational: not of the mind but of the soul, not thought out, not reasoned. This is the 'red mist' we often hear people say they felt at times they lost rational control of themselves; *orgē* is thought out, *thumos* is thoughtless!

Thumos is the less common one and is rendered in the NIV (with the exception of Revelation) as 'rage' or 'fits of rage'. *Orgē* is translated as both 'anger' and 'wrath' and where we read of the 'wrath of God', it is *orgē* in the gospels and letters. The exception in Revelation is that the wrath of God there is *thumos*, but this is apocalyptic literature and very different in its message and its aims. We could try to state that if God can be righteous and feel such wrath, then it must not be sinful, but in the same way that judging people is his preserve and not ours, then we cannot take on this attribute glibly and try to fool ourselves that we are still being righteous. We know that vengeance is forbidden for us to take, and we are to leave that to God (Rom. 12:19, referring to Deut. 32:35). So, the question remains… **can** we be angry, and if so, where do we draw the line over which we should not tread?

Seeing the difficulties and wishing to get through them, let us return to Paul, who told the Ephesians *"In your anger, do not sin."* He later exhorts them to *"Get rid of all… rage (thumos) and anger (orgē),…."* (4:31), so why seem to separate anger from sin in v.26, then tell us to get rid of rage **and** anger? Paul repeats this list of things we are to disassociate ourselves from, in four of his letters, to the Corinthians, Galatians, Ephesians and Colossians:

> *For I am afraid that when I come I may not find you as I want you to be, and you may not find me as you want me to be. I fear that there may be discord, jealousy, fits of rage, selfish ambition, slander, gossip, arrogance and disorder.* (2Cor. 12:20)

The acts of the flesh are obvious: sexual immorality, impurity and debauchery; idolatry and witchcraft; hatred, discord, jealousy, <u>fits of rage</u>, selfish ambition, dissensions, factions and envy; drunkenness, orgies, and the like. I warn you, as I did before, that those who live like this will not inherit the kingdom of God. (Gal. 5:19-21)

Get rid of all bitterness, <u>rage and anger</u>, brawling and slander, along with every form of malice. (Eph. 4:31)

But now you must also rid yourselves of all such things as these: <u>anger, rage</u>, malice, slander, and filthy language from your lips. (Col. 3:8)
[underlining my own]

In the last two examples, he includes anger (*orgē*) along with rage (*thumos*), yet in the first two, anger is not present. Why the differences? The only thing I can discern is found in the **context** (remember that maxim?). The letters to the Corinthians and the Galatians are warnings about other false teachers - in Corinth, some had come trying to undermine Paul's apostolic authority and turn the church from his teaching, while in Galatia, legalist Judaisers were attempting to take them back to observance of ceremonial law. Paul himself is angry in these letters, and trying to deal with dangerous doctrine; he takes on the rôle of prophet, proclaiming to them just what is truly dangerous and what they **must** turn from, or they "*will not inherit the kingdom of God.*" Strong words indeed!

However, the letters to the Ephesians and the Colossians have a much more 'pastoral' tone to them. He is offering kind advice and instruction on how to live as better saints and pointing out the things they would benefit from by avoiding, and anger, the 'rational' *orgē*, **is** included. This occupies a lower ranking than *thumos* for Paul: not something that will keep them from the kingdom, or detract from their salvation, but best avoided if they want to live holy and walk in true righteousness. In fact, 'anger' in Eph. 4:26 (*In your anger do not sin*) is **not** *orgē*, but *orgizo*, which is the verb, not the noun - a better translation of this is "*If you **get** angry, do not sin*" (MOUNCE) [emphasis mine]. Paul seems to be understanding that we **do** get angry, and often justifiably so; he **does** get angry addressing the Corinthians and Galatians, but he exhorts us that our best effort is to turn from it quickly, before it leads us to sin, before we lose control and give in to the flaming *thumos*. James also counsels us:

> *My dear brothers and sisters, take note of this: Everyone should be quick to listen, slow to speak and slow to become angry, because human anger does not produce the righteousness that God desires.* (James 1:19-20)

God's anger

There is a wholly different and actually disconnected debate about God's acts 'of wrath' that I have shifted on over the years since I began writing this. This was never a 'denial of truth' but a recognition that I had not been reading scripture in a proper way. Some will say that God is not wrathful at all and there is a lot to be said for the argument; nowhere is God described as wrath in the same way as '*God is love*' (1Jn. 4:8). As a father I can agree that I am entitled to become angry with my children if they misbehave... wrathful? Not so! So if God is my good Father, my perfect Father, then I can see how some things might anger him, but I know that he is '*slow to anger and abounding in love*' (Ex. 34:6, Num. 14:18, Neh. 9:17, Ps. 86:15, 103:8, 145:8, Joel 2:13, Jon. 4:2) - note how often this phrase is repeated through the OT, and yet trying to 'downplay' the wrath of God could lead to me being accused of being a Marcionite by someone somewhere - it's de rigeur for theologians!

Marcion (85-160AD), like many others, questioned how a 'God of love' can also be a 'God of wrath' and suggested these are incompatible, even mutually exclusive i.e. he cannot be both! Marcion used this 'reasoning' to lead him to the heresy that the god of the OT is not the god of the NT and Jesus! This attempt to think out God's character could be labelled an example of trying to anthropomorphise God - just a long word that means trying to attribute human characteristics to something: Mickey Mouse is an anthropomorphised mouse who walks upright on two legs, and so an anthropomorphised God will look more like us and less like him! We are made in **his** image; when we make him in **our** image, we become humanists!

There is so much wrong here; first, Marcion is choosing to ignore all those references in the OT of God's love. The Hebrew word for love there is the well-known '*[c]hesed*' that means 'everlasting love' and can also mean mercy, but is marked in its description of a merciful love that is practically boundless and beyond our comprehension.

Marcion claimed that he was a disciple of Paul, who he saw as the only real apostle, and limited his canon to the Pauline letters. However, Paul reasons in Romans about just how this OT 'God of wrath' actually held off on his wrath "*with great patience*" against sinful humans in waiting for the redemption to come for Jew and Gentile alike (Rom. 9:22-29). Therefore I have always shied from those 'street preachers' with megaphones who walked around talking about nothing but this wrathful God who was rubbing his hands with glee, ready to chuck all the unbelievers into eternal fire (or was that just on the streets of Belfast?) - **my** bible emphasises the **love** of God, and his patience and **reluctance** to judge, not his joy! Paul clearly preached **that** God of mercy from his scriptures (our OT).

Second, to level the accusation of 'Marcionite' at anyone who tries to dispel the 'God of wrath' image is so ironic because it's this dual view of a schizophrenic God that leads to the ideas that **are** Marcionism. Once you recognise that anger is only one of the attributes of an immensely loving God, whose mercy is beyond our understanding, that you realise what he meant when he said '*my ways are not your ways*' (Is. 55:8) - this really has more to do with how he forgives so readily, unlike us, who hold grudges and take time to forgive. This brings us to the third conclusion: just because **we**, as mortal creations, are given to wrath, and very capable of acting or speaking before we think or reason things out, that does not mean that God is the same; that's **our** anthropomorphising! Sorry for the big word.

We have one more thing to consider here, though; the controversial passage about Jesus clearing the Temple. It is controversial since it flies in the face of the 'meek' Jesus, the one we've been reading about who condemned anger (and, as we shall see, preached non-violence and the 'turn the other cheek' philosophy - how do we equate it with his actions here? There are accounts of the event in all four gospels, though Matthew (21:12-13) and Luke (19:45-46) only mention it very briefly. We have more detail in Mark and John:

> *On reaching Jerusalem, Jesus entered the temple courts and began driving out those who were buying and selling there. He overturned the tables of the money changers and the benches of those selling doves, and would not allow anyone to carry merchandise through the temple courts. And as he taught them, he said, "Is it not written: 'My house will be called a house of prayer for all nations'? But you have made it 'a den of robbers.'* (Mark 11:15-17)

> *When it was almost time for the Jewish Passover, Jesus went up to Jerusalem. In the temple courts he found people selling cattle, sheep and doves, and others sitting at tables exchanging money. So he made a whip out of cords, and drove all from the temple courts, both sheep and cattle; he scattered the coins of the money changers and overturned their tables. To those who sold doves he said, "Get these out of here! Stop turning my Father's house into a market!" His disciples remembered that it is written: "Zeal for your house will consume me."* (John 2: 13-17)

Some commentators have sought to say that these two accounts relate to two separate events since they would appear to be at different times chronologically, but the gospels were not written with an exact detail to timeline in the way we would seek, so I cannot think of this happening twice; it is a one-off occurrence, which stands out as certainly different from the usual behaviour of our Lord Jesus. We read in both accounts that he overturned tables and drove people out. It has long been 'accepted' that Jesus was violently angry here, but we need to read the accounts carefully. John tells us that he made a whip to do this, while Mark makes no mention of a whip. However, note that he says that he *drove all from the temple courts, both sheep and cattle* - the 'all' being driven with the whip were just the sheep and cattle! **Not** the people! Many might say it would be hard to imagine, reading Mark's account, just how he could drive anyone out **without** such an instrument, but there is no written account of him actually **striking** anyone, so how can we read 'into' this that such a thing happened? When driving out 'both sheep and cattle', it's actually the crack of a whip that will scare the animals into fleeing without any actual striking. Could this have been the same method to clear the people? Jesus would have known that he would not have to actually strike anyone, but he was angry enough to scare them. It seems to me that implying our Lord was violent towards them is in someone's agenda; to justify such violence in us! How could we find our Lord behaving violently? All four gospel writers record for us that the servant of the High Priest had his ear cut off in Gethsemane by Peter, whom Jesus immediately rebuked (Matt. 26:51; Mark 14:47; Luke 22:50; John 18:10), so if such physical violence occurred in the Temple here, we may conclude fairly safely that it would have been reported. My conclusion has to be that he did not use violence on anyone, not even the animals. He was just angry enough to frighten them into getting out of the place. I have also seen this verse taken out of context to excuse violence - right before his arrest: *He said to them, 'But now if you have a purse, take it, and also a bag; and if you don't have a sword, sell your cloak and buy one.* (Luke 22:36) You only have to read what Jesus said in the next verses!

> I*t is written: "And he was numbered with the transgressors"; and I tell you that this must be fulfilled in me. Yes, what is written about me is reaching its fulfilment.'*
> *The disciples said, 'See, Lord, here are two swords.'*
> *'That's enough!' he replied.* (37, 38)

So he only wanted to fulfil that scripture (Is. 53:12), and two swords were enough. To defend against the whole of the Temple Guard!? When Peter actually did use his sword and cut off someone's ear, Jesus stopped them immediately, healed the ear, and made it clear: *all who draw the sword will die by the sword.* (Matt. 26:52)

For me, the key to the clearing of the Temple is what John attributes to his disciples, when later on they recall Psalm 69:9, a single verse out of a fairly long Psalm (36 verses) that is a psalm of despair and anger, where the writer David calls the Lord to vindicate and defend him against the taunts and accusations of his enemies. In the midst of this long woe-fest, David proclaims:

for zeal for your house consumes me,
and the insults of those who insult you fall on me.
When I weep and fast,
I must endure scorn;
when I put on sackcloth,
people make sport of me. (9-11)

To put this in context, David has a passion for God and his house, and seeks his lord in humility (weeping, fasting, wearing sackcloth) but for this he just gets scorn from others, who wish to mock him for his pious spirituality. He himself cannot take any sort of retribution from them or redress them so he asks God to do it for him; he hands over the rôle of judge and arbiter of justice to him. The key word for us is *zeal*: in this context it is positive, and expresses a right heart that is consumed with a passion for the things of God, but does not wish to exact its own revenge on the scoffers. Zeal, though, is not always positive. Paul recalls to the Philippians that he had a zeal for persecuting the church before his conversion (Phil. 3:6), that false teachers may have zeal *"to win you over, but for no good... that you may have zeal for them"* (Gal. 4:17), and zeal can be misguided e.g. the Israelites *"are zealous for God, but their zeal is not based on knowledge"* (Rom. 10:2). Paul does exhort us to zeal, yes, but for the right things:

Never be lacking in zeal, but keep your spiritual fervour, serving the Lord. (Rom. 12:11)

It is fine to be zealous, provided the purpose is good, and to be so always, not just when I am with you. (Gal. 4:18)

This zeal, or passion, is certainly similar to anger; it can be aroused in a good way, and consume us with all that our love for God can muster within us, but if misplaced or applied incorrectly, it can be dangerous. Jesus' zeal for the house of the Lord, the Temple, was applied by him in perfection, since he is perfect. Who else can say that such zeal will always be applied so perfectly? Might we simply say on this: God is able to be angry without sinning, just as he alone is able, as we have determined, to judge properly.

I think that the clearest thing to take from this is that Jesus certainly **did** get angry, and that anger that he expressed, usually in words, was directed at those who made gain from religion, whether it was financial profit, or power and prestige, or just a desire to have people listening to their 'teachings'. Following God should never be about what profit can be made. I only heard this week of a pastor who was presented with a plan to create and equip a youth centre in his church costing £12,000 and his instant reply was "how will we make this back?" That pastor was a former businessman, so his mindset was on costs and 'efficiency' - the High Priest at the Temple would likely make the same argument that a profit had to be made for the running of the Temple and the maintenance of the priesthood, but Jesus was having none of it, obviously. Should we not then also get angry at this?

We still have a problem, though. If we are looking at anger as something best avoided, something that easily leads us into sin, just as Jesus has warned us that this is equivalent to murder, then how are we to look up to Jesus as our example, when he allowed himself to get angry in this physical way? If we consider that he did **not** actually strike anyone with his whip, then we must ask if he might not have known if anyone would have tried to stand up to him and forced him to actually use it. However, his knowledge of events and situations was far beyond anything **we** could know; it would be very presumptive of any of us, fallen sinful individuals that we are, to take up a similar physical stance and believe we would not have to get violent in some way. Let us view this incident as one that was within our Lord's own knowledge and control, as was everything he did - he even went to the cross in full knowledge of the master plan! (John 10:18), and the Father was with him: *"But if I do judge, my decisions are true, because I am not alone."* (John 8:16). We may well be allowed to become angry at certain things, and we should be careful to only get angry at those things that anger **him**, but this should be reserved, controlled, and brief; we should be *quick to listen, slow to speak and slow to become angry* and turn from it before we fall into rage. Oh, I must learn this over again and again! If anger is such a dangerous thing for us, and too easily leads us into error and sinful actions, then let us seek to be content with pursuing a peaceful existence that avoids anger and runs from it when it is detected within ourselves. We will revisit this when looking at insults in Part 3.

I am reminded of a great poem by William Blake that we read at school. It explains how we can choose to embrace or reject wrath when it occurs, and maybe see just when and why we make such a choice:

A Poison Tree

I was angry with my friend;
I told my wrath, my wrath did end.

I was angry with my foe:
I told it not, my wrath did grow.

And I waterd it in fears,
Night & morning with my tears:
And I sunned it with smiles,
And with soft deceitful wiles.

And it grew both day and night.
Till it bore an apple bright.
And my foe beheld it shine,
And he knew that it was mine.

And into my garden stole,
When the night had veild the pole;
In the morning glad I see;
My foe outstretched beneath the tree.

After discussing the fruit of the 'tree of judgment', I am
captivated by Blake's metaphor of his wrath as an apple!
Blake is honest to admit that he makes such distinctions
between friends and foes, but Jesus shall even dispel this
when we get to his last '*but I tell you...*' command!

Adultery

You have heard that it was said, "You shall not
commit adultery." But I tell you that anyone who
looks at a woman lustfully has already committed
adultery with her in his heart. If your right eye
causes you to stumble, gouge it out and throw it
away. It is better for you to lose one part of your
body than for your whole body to be thrown into

hell. And if your right hand causes you to stumble, cut it off and throw it away. It is better for you to lose one part of your body than for your whole body to go into hell.

The second '*but I tell you…*' deals with adultery, and again, takes it beyond the mere act of infidelity against one's spouse. In addressing adultery, I hear Jesus making it very plain to me: "you may say that you have never cheated on your wife, and remained faithful to her, but if you have ever even looked at another woman in the wrong way… there, in your heart, is your sin. NO! I do not approve!" I **would** be a fool and a liar, and worthy of being labelled so by everyone, were I to say that I have never done that. There are so many sexy images of women all around us, and so many beautiful young women that turn my middle-aged head. There's nothing wrong with noticing someone attractive. I can even say to my wife on occasion that were I half my age and single, I might well be pursuing a certain single woman, and she would agree that said single woman is attractive and more importantly, a very nice person. Going from thinking 'she's attractive!' to having lewd thoughts about what might lie beneath her clothing is not a hurdle or a fence but simply a line in the sand that I can choose easily to step over. I have seen a woman walk into a room and turn many other men's heads, so I know I am not alone. I have also seen women blush when a handsome young hunk says 'hello' so I challenge the women to refute me on that one too! Jesus even tells us in this passage that if our eye 'causes us to stumble' in this matter, we should 'gouge it out and throw it away'!! Strong words again! These admonitions are also very difficult for us to accept since we live in a world that has a pervasive secular view of things that has dismissed the spiritual and the pursuit of God, and so reduced sin to 'bad behaviour' and defines it by saying "what doesn't hurt anyone else is **my** business alone, and cannot be bad since there are no consequences for anyone else!" Is this Jesus' view of sin? From his sermon, it would certainly seem not! A book I enjoyed reading just recently was "The Myth of the Christian Religion" by Greg Boyd. A few chapters in Boyd's book seemed not to be applicable to me, but on reading, I saw how wrong my assumptions were. His chapter on secularism turned out to be the most radical for me since I had no idea just how much secularism had invaded my thinking, yet we live our lives every day in a perpetual state of going after the things that we are told we must pursue; money, work, pleasure, comfort, etc. and we scantly pay attention to God and his plans and his leading for us except when we go to a church meeting and then for an hour or so we try to focus on him, though it's difficult to maintain this when we have so many other things on our minds while we are there! However, his chapter on 'the revolt against the abuse of sex' is apt for many of us in the 21st century Western world where so much sexual imagery is used to even sell products and promote business, and so much warped thinking about sexuality that goes against the monogamous ideal appears on our TV screens via everyday sitcoms and soaps, we certainly need to keep a clear and 'clean' picture in our minds of what God desires for us to think. Those of us who may count ourselves 'spiritual' may spend a portion of the day in prayer regularly, but this itself may not be enough to protect our minds from 'worldly thinking' throughout the rest of the day. Boyd asks us to do meditations, by focusing our minds on a picture of Christ showing his hands to us and telling us how he loves us, or of the cross where he was hanging to die. These pictures can help us to fill our minds with clear visualisations of a representation of our Lord and the beauty of his loving sacrifice for us, thus making it much harder for thoughts to occur that may not be conducive to our spirituality. Note that I did not say 'enter' since I do not believe that thoughts enter our minds - **ideas**, and primarily **images** (which can be more instant in their effect), may enter our mind; how we deal with them then becomes our thoughts, and they are ours alone. A continuous quest to keep images and thoughts about God freshly in our minds can **only** help in this fight, this inner struggle.

> *Finally, brothers and sisters, whatever is true, whatever is noble, whatever is right, whatever is pure, whatever is lovely, whatever is admirable—if anything is excellent or praiseworthy—think about such things.* (Phil. 4:8)

What could be **more** noble, true, right, pure, lovely… than Jesus himself?

I shall not enter into any debate here about 'appropriate dress' that many Christians fall into, since this distracts me from my own problem. If I look lustfully at another woman, how she dresses has nothing to do with it! It is addressed to me by my Lord, directly, and he never qualifies it with a "but if **she** has dressed in such a way that distracts a man…" - he addresses the sin within each and every one of us, which is owned by each person, on their own. **Don't blame others for your shortcomings!**

I recall a great book I read as a young believer called "Celebration of Discipline" by Richard Foster - meditation was the first discipline to be addressed; it is something we have rejected in the west since we associate it with eastern Transcendental Meditation, yet it was a discipline within Christian tradition for centuries, and has great value for spiritual life. While Boyd talks of pictures to bring to mind regularly throughout our daily life, Foster was more concerned with the discipline of meditation on specific scripture verses and scriptural truths to dwell on them and mull over every single word and its meaning to us, thus finding new things within it while prayerfully asking God to assist our understanding. Let us be mindful of how much we need to guard against wrong imagery and thinking within ourselves in the context of what Christ is teaching us here, in this, his seminal 'kingdom living' lesson.

So, in the addressing of murder and adultery, we need to ask if Jesus is saying that wrong attitudes and secret thoughts from our head actually constitute 'thoughtcrime' long before George Orwell coined that phrase in '1984'? It is interesting to note that this term has been used to discuss those who offer ideas contrary to a received theology (and so ironically apt in my opinion). Can it be that such hidden opinions and images that Jesus addressed are genuinely 'sin' in God's eyes?

To go back to the Tree of Judgment and relate it to these issues Jesus raised in his sermon; we now have a very good explanation of what he was trying to convey; for **us**, murder does not equate to name-calling and judging, nor does adultery equate to lewd thoughts, and we set laws to distinguish penalties for one and not the other (just as they were set by Moses for the people of Israel leaving Egypt to create their own society and nation). However, this is within **our** understanding. God has a different standard: **all** these things are wrong in his eyes, and this call of Jesus is to attain to that higher standard. Surely, though, such a standard is unattainable? Boyd, in his chapter 'The Revolt Against Judgment' describes what he calls 'mental gossip' which he became aware of while sitting in a shopping mall waiting for his wife (a man I can relate to - "bookstores and music shops excepted, shopping is boring!!" - my own paraphrase of his words, but I concur wholeheartedly). Something I am sure every single one of us will be aware we do, and do constantly; is having internal thoughts about people you see passing by e.g. "She calls **that** a dress? More like a tea towel!", "You wouldn't catch **me** giving in to that spoilt child so easily!", "I'd not let **my** wife talk to me like that: Pathetic man!" Any of that sound familiar? Whether you have voiced such thoughts openly or not, I would challenge **anyone** to claim that they **never** entertain such thoughts internally! Let's just say that you actually never do voice them to anyone else, and you can feel perfectly self-righteous about that, but hold on! What have we been reading about what Jesus was teaching his followers (us!)? Such judgmental thoughts are **still** wrong, sinful, forbidden, denounced, rejected, **completely** by our Lord. Even when they are internal and unvoiced! Jesus does not reserve condemnation in these admonitions for actions alone, no! He condemns **being** angry with a brother or sister, and **thinking** a lewd thought about someone; voicing and actions are not a factor - he evaluates the wrong **thoughts**, in my head and yours, as sin! If, right now, you are thinking to yourself "no, Jesus couldn't possibly have meant that just as it sounds, surely?" then you are in a place I've been in too. Some of the things that Jesus taught truly **are** difficult to swallow; we, in our human nature, and influenced by the world around us (even I, a free-thinking misfit, will admit to that!), seek to find an escape hatch, a way out, and try to explain it away with 'logic' or 'common sense' - such things may fit into **our** minds, but not his. He requires **obedience**, pure and simple. Judging is a thought that occurs in our head, as is getting angry with someone (since we have judged them as 'worthy' of our anger), or thinking lewd thoughts about someone (since we have judged ourselves as able to think such things about another human being).

Sheesh! This Jesus following business is getting even harder, eh? I could never manage to keep to these standards. Could you? How? I saw a graph for usage of gym membership over the months of a year, put up on Facebook for a laugh. Of course, January has the highest peak, decreasing over the year to maybe a short peak before the summer months (must get back into that swimsuit!). We all know why. How many New Year's resolutions last into February, really? This is a familiar trait of what we call 'human nature' and unfortunately when it is carried over into church, it can be disastrous. We make appeals to the lost to 'come to Jesus' but we may allow new converts to fall into this trap of 'good intention' if we portray the picture of 'instant change' on the day we said 'the sinner's prayer' (that **is** the 'standard evangelical testimony', isn't it?); they discover fairly readily that the sin in their lives doesn't all just go away in a flash and they start to think of themselves as unworthy of following Christ, or just not cut out for church life, like an athlete who doesn't make the cut for the olympic team. Suffice to say that this discontentment over remaining imperfection in the young believer may well be the first disgruntlement we all experience. My experience of finding so many who've fallen away from faith ('backsliders' was a term we use to describe them) in my native East Belfast leads me to think that we need to be honest about these shortcomings in all of us, especially to help new believers understand the nature of true contentment in the Christian life. Since we know that that 'first joy' (which Keith Green sang about so eloquently in "When I First Trusted You") does not last, we should help them find something more lasting. We can look at the example of the great apostle Paul, pioneer of the faith, in one of his later epistles where he laid out the way of Jesus and his grace in that theological masterpiece to the Romans, and take encouragement that he suffered the same too! Here's just a snippet of his inner rant in chapter 7:

> *We know that the law is spiritual; but I am unspiritual, sold as a slave to sin. I do not understand what I do. For what I want to do I do not do, but what I hate I do. And if I do what I do not want to do, I agree that the law is good. As it is, it is no longer I myself who do it, but it is sin living in me. For I know that good itself does not dwell in me, that is, in my sinful nature. For I have the desire to do what is good, but I cannot carry it out. For I do not do the good I want to do, but the evil I do not want to do – this I keep on doing. Now if I do what I do not want to do, it is no longer I who do it, but it is sin living in me that does it.*
> (Romans 7:14-20)

Yet, despite this inner turmoil, Paul was also the author of such brilliantly quotable pieces like this, concluding his rant:

> *Therefore, there is now no condemnation for those who are in Christ Jesus, because through Christ Jesus the law of the Spirit who gives life has set you free from the law of sin and death.* (Romans 8:1,2)

How do we get to this place where Paul gets to, despite his knowing that he still is this imperfect disciple? I hope you can come with me on this examination and find a simple answer, even if there are different parts to it. One of the elements then, is certainly perseverance. Paul knew that. If we give up too easily, we undermine the grace extended to us. Much like some newly-weds find the 'lovey-dovey' feelings they had don't stay the course, and true love and commitment is required for the long haul: the inability to find that deep devotion to each other may well be the major factor in many short marriages. So it is with 'loving Christ', I believe. This brings us neatly to the next issue…

Divorce

> *It has been said, 'Anyone who divorces his wife must give her a certificate of divorce.' But I tell you that anyone who divorces his wife, except for sexual immorality, makes her the victim of adultery, and anyone who marries a divorced woman commits adultery.*

After setting out a definition for adultery that is within our hearts, Jesus then states that the actual practice of adultery is the **only** grounds for divorce, despite an allowance for it outside that restriction **within the law**. He refers to a law in Deuteronomy 24:1 where a man was allowed to divorce a wife *"who becomes displeasing to him because he finds something indecent about her"* (NIV). The Hebrew translated as 'indecent' in the NIV is *ervah*, which the KJV renders 'uncleanness' but actually comes from a root that means 'nakedness' and is translated elsewhere in the OT as most often 'naked/ -ness'. I shall refrain from going into a lengthy commentary about this here, but from our 21st century perspective, can we not feel some revulsion about how women were treated in this way in what is called 'God's law'? So a man was able to just say that he found something about her that was 'indecent' or 'unclean' and present her with a certificate and send her away? The accusation that OT law was full of misogyny (hatred of women) is **very** hard to refute on the evidence (and this is only the tip of the inherent problems!). However, Jesus stands and denounces this, and overturns it! Yes? What was he saying earlier about 'not the smallest letter… will by any means disappear from the Law until everything is accomplished'? How do we get around this? As a male Israelite, I could refer to the law and say "I'm divorcing my wife. Don't like her anymore. Here's her certificate" but Jesus is saying 'no' to that, and that the **only** grounds for divorce is 'sexual immorality' and any other reason actually **makes** her a 'victim of adultery' as well as the next man who marries her! Thankfully, we can investigate this further since later some Pharisees pulled him up on it:

> *Some Pharisees came to him to test him. They asked, "Is it lawful for a man to divorce his wife for any and every reason?"*

"Haven't you read," he replied, "that at the beginning the Creator 'made them male and female,' and said, 'For this reason a man will leave his father and mother and be united to his wife, and the two will become one flesh'? So they are no longer two, but one flesh. Therefore what God has joined together, let no one separate."

"Why then," they asked, "did Moses command that a man give his wife a certificate of divorce and send her away?"

Jesus replied, "Moses permitted you to divorce your wives because your hearts were hard. But it was not this way from the beginning. I tell you that anyone who divorces his wife, except for sexual immorality, and marries another woman commits adultery." (Matt.19:3-9)

Matthew Henry, in his commentary, tries to explain this by pointing out that the Pharisees saw this particular law as a precept (another word for a commandment). Henry is correct; they thought of it as something Moses laid down to command them, once they were displeased with their wife, to make out the bill of divorce, but this is a common mistake made by those who apply overly stringent reading of their scriptures, as if every word is a command to be followed. It has been used to defend slavery and demean women's suffrage (and in some quarters, it still is!). In this case, we have a particular allowance that Moses inserted, which was gleefully used by men who wished to dismiss a wife for whatever reason they needed. Note that Jesus clearly identified who wrote that law! They were misinterpreting it anyway, even if it wasn't a command from God, and this is also a major problem in every generation. I hope we can get to the nub of what Jesus said on this mountain.

> [We need to be mindful of what I mentioned earlier; that in Jesus' time, Hebrew had died as a language in common usage, and been superseded by Aramaic, which is similar to Hebrew, but no more than German is to English, so the Pharisees were not native speakers of the Hebrew of their scriptures, though they would have learnt it well at rabbinical school. Their understanding of the words of the law would be non-native and a fair few centuries out too. Since native speakers of all the Biblical languages no longer exist, translation can be a real minefield.]

While avoiding a detailed debate about the nature of the Mosaic Law, we need to grasp just what Jesus is meaning here. For him, there was a standard **before** the law, and it was a standard for any individual who loved the Lord, and it was certainly, **again**, a higher standard! Moses gave these hard-hearted Israelite men **permission** to divorce, so it wasn't a misunderstanding over words and was originally a limit on the grounds; Moses actually allowed the people, who were about to go into Canaan and set up their new nation, to forego this principle that God had established with Adam and Eve, and be allowed to divorce if they so wished! No, scrub 'people' - it was for the men! Those accusations of misogyny seem to gain a little bit of weight now, don't they?

What is Jesus doing, though? After talking about murder and adultery, he throws in a piece about divorce; is this relevant? Yes, once you grasp how important the marriage of one person with another is, in the eyes of God, you see how this fits in perfectly with the narrative, which is a narrative of LOVE, after all. One of the stranger books in the scriptures that comprise our OT now, is the Song of Songs (or Song of Solomon). It is ascribed to Solomon as a 'book of wisdom' and while it makes no mention of God and is purely a love poem between two lovers, which is actually **quite** erotic if you take the time to read it (a pastor I sat under for many years refused to ever preach from it), the perceived wisdom has always been that it is a metaphor, or picture, of the deep love that God has for his people, his church. Indeed, much of what Jesus taught in his parables involved a bride and bridegroom, which reflects the use of 'bride' throughout the Song of Songs. This picture shows us the deep love that Jesus has for his church, and how some scripture likens his return as for a young woman waiting to be his bride; **we** are the bride anticipating the wedding. Rachel Held Evans covered this metaphor wonderfully in her book 'Searching for Sunday' so I'll defer to her if you want to explore that any further. Jesus was making it clear to the Pharisees, and also to all his listeners here, that a man needs to love his wife properly, and not view her as a possession. If we can't do this for a spouse, how will we ever get to that difficult 'love everyone including your enemies' bit?

However, since divorce among Christians is practically rampant compared to what I observed around me only 20 years ago, there **must** be a practical principle that we can take from this. Is it possible that this is one area in which the world around us has also 'hardened our hearts'? In

Boyd's terms, we must revolt against the abuse of relationship.

Let me explain; a good friend of mine, who is now a minister, told me some years ago that he was sitting watching one of our most popular 'soaps' on TV, in which a female character had been suffering in her marriage to a boorish and uncaring man. She found someone else, more loving and understanding, and clearly longed to be rid of the husband she had grown to despise, but in a heated debate with the man she married, she seemed to lack the will to just let go of her vows. My friend then shouted at the screen; "just divorce him, love!" Immediately he was struck with conviction: was he advocating that someone should just give up on a marriage at the first sign of a 'better option'? He realised right away how the soap fiction had drawn him into a bad territory of wrong thinking about what marriage is about. Personally, I **do** believe that anyone who abuses a spouse in any way, is in danger of being told rightly that their behaviour is a breach of their vows and that **they** are the ones who have pushed away such a spouse who seeks to end their union. I certainly would never agree that anyone being physically abused should remain in a marital home; they should be removed and protected, by all and any means! Yet I have heard of such a case where church elders, aware of the problem, told a wife to "just try harder to be a good wife"!!! So while we want to be aware of how outside influences can draw us away from what Christ taught us, we also need to be wise in deciphering and interpreting his words. The question is this; if Jesus was challenging the accepted religious norm of his day about divorce, would he do the same today? I really would like to think that any of my readers would agree that a physically-abused spouse should have the right to divorce the abuser, if no progress could be made on them to overcome the abuse, through counselling. Right away, I know of objectors who would draw us back to Jesus' words and say that unless adultery has occurred, divorce is not possible. Is this not falling into the same trap as the Pharisees? Can we not determine in Jesus a desire to move forward from such thinking? His plea is to treat one another in love, and would binding an abused person to a marriage (even if that is one lived in absence from the abuser) with no permission to find a better spouse, not be an act of cruelty? The oft repeated mantra 'What Would Jesus Do?' should be applied to more things than we **want** to apply it to. For anyone in such a situation, the words of Jesus might ring out to them that except for sexual immorality, they are not to divorce! If such a believer can then become content with their situation, that is up to them. In essence, they might accept that their marriage vows are unbreakable and quit grumbling about their lot? Much prayer must be done, and much good counselling should be sought in these cases, and a final decision should be left to each person, without judgment on the part of any other. The only judge is God, in the end, and how a believer reacts to these words of our Lord Jesus is a matter for them to reconcile and be answerable for.

I can hear the objection; "that's moral relativism!" which is the charge that we cannot apply commands and laws differently to each individual, but in the spirit of Paul's argument in Romans 14, each believer **does** have a choice on some matters that cannot be imposed by others. The spouse who has been systematically abused and neglected by an unloving partner deserves a lot more sympathy than the one who, say, decides that they want to pursue another career in a foreign country and leaves their spouse to pursue their own 'happiness' so each case is different, but the spirit of love, commitment and perseverance should be over all of it. I shall reiterate that for anyone in such a state, a personal decision must be made based on all the facts peculiar to their situation, with no fear of judgment - I put forward that if God could 'allow' Moses a get-out clause for men who were acting like unsatisfied customers, surely he can make allowances for your particular pain? Also, for anyone who knows another in such a state, I would advise that you cannot make a decision for them or offer any particular advice either way (unless they are being abused and need intervention); be careful you do not help them make a wrong decision! This is an issue fraught with difficulties, especially when you have a personal vested interest, like with a close family member. The modern western view that divorce happens to anyone and we should just accept it as an unfortunate feature of life is wrong from what should be our stance on the commands of our Lord, but the other end of the scale where women were expected to put up with just about anything since they were viewed as possessions by some men is equally wrong. Maybe even more so, since this is the attitude Jesus was addressing with not just the Pharisees, but his entire original audience on that Mount! He provides his declarations about commitment in a loving covenant between two people to reiterate how committed he is to his own bride, the church i.e. us! In learning about this most intimate and exclusive relationship, we become more aware of our relationship with him. After all, it **is** all about relationship, not religion, isn't it?

The main lesson to take from this particular command of Jesus is this, though: The individual who chooses to follow Christ must know that they are called to a higher standard than any law given for the administration of a society. Such laws, whether given by man or God, whether allowed by God or not, do not constitute that which we are called to be. We must strive to be better, higher, grander in our pursuit of holiness than the Law prescribes or even allows. It is the very power of the gospel, the same power that sets us free, that also empowers us to achieve this. In this journey, we shall hopefully arrive at what this means and how we can achieve or maintain such standards... can we?

> *"The law of Moses considered the hardness of men's hearts, but the gospel of Christ cures it."*
>
> - Matthew Henry

Oaths

> *Again, you have heard that it was said to the people long ago, 'Do not break your oath, but fulfil to the Lord the vows you have made.' But I tell you, do not swear an oath at all: either by heaven, for it is God's throne; or by the earth, for it is his footstool; or by Jerusalem, for it is the city of the Great King. And do not swear by your head, for you cannot make even one hair white or black. All you need to say is simply 'Yes' or 'No'; anything beyond this comes from the evil one.*

Jesus then deals with the making of oaths. There are a number of references within the Mosaic law to oaths and vows but most of them are instructions for ceremonial vows surrounding sacrificial practice. They are in practically all cases binding upon the swearer of the oath. There would seem to be two cases where such undertakings **can** be dissolved. In Numbers 30, provisions are made for women - unmarried women making vows to God can have them annulled by their father, and married women by their husbands (widows and divorced women are exempt from this control). Yet more proof that some of the provisions of the law were to appease men, since it seems absurd to me that a vow to God could be overruled by a man, but there you are!

The other provision is very interesting for our purposes here, though. In Leviticus 4 & 5, we have a long passage that allows for 'unintentional sins' e.g. touching an unclean thing by accident, or realising later that a certain law had been broken, and the various sin offerings that should be made. Amongst this is *or if anyone thoughtlessly takes an oath to do anything, whether good or evil (in any matter one might carelessly swear about) even though they are unaware of it, but then they learn of it and realise their guilt— when anyone becomes aware that they are guilty in any of these matters, they must confess in what way they have sinned.* (5:4-5), which then prescribes the appropriate sacrificial action to take. What exactly is happening here? It would appear that it addresses 'careless swearing', from the wording '*any matter one might carelessly swear about*'. It's only a facet of human nature that we can all make such sudden irresponsible declarations, like "I swear to God that I'm going to resign my job first thing tomorrow!" Once one has recovered from the moment of madness and realises their folly, such an 'oath' becomes meaningless. More often, in fact, such utterances have become so familiar they are a case of a change in our language where they have become meaningless by default, and they trip off our tongues without much thought and have no actual validity as 'oaths'! Like "I swear to God; if he says that once more, I'll slap him!" or "I swear I'm going to kill her!" when the maker of these has no genuine intention to carry it through (usually!). However, in a culture where words have power and such swearing by something sacred or holy, such as the name of God, is seen as binding upon the utterer, rash proclamations like these need to be 'undone' by repentance and sacrifice. We as Christians should certainly be aware of this too, since many of these things should be reverenced by us too. I see this as the true meaning of 'taking the Lord's name in vain' and it should not be used so lightly or without attention to how inappropriate it might be to invoke it. Many Christians get annoyed at non-believers who use 'God' and 'Jesus' as pure exclamations or 'mild' swear words and say that people shouldn't take those names 'in vain' - I used to be one who did get annoyed at this. I would have others who might say the f-word or the c-word in my presence and then say "oh sorry, you're a Christian, aren't you?" then go ahead and use 'Jesus' multiple times. Now, for me, if I take the attitude that for them the names hold no real significance and they utter them without much thought at all, then it is much easier to ignore them and not get so annoyed. For **us**, they hold meaning so let us reverence them appropriately and simply be content that others are not blaspheming in any way as such, but are themselves ignorant of this flippancy; we can pray for them to come to know the truth, and the real meaning of this, yet determine that we will maintain such reverence in our lives if we wish to do so, and not hound them over something that, **to them,** is of little consequence. Otherwise we may find our anger rising day by day; pray for a spirit of peace in this.

Right away though, in this Levitical provision for unintended oaths, we have a provision in the law for such a 'thoughtcrime', or more aptly a 'lack-of-thoughtcrime' - it formed in your head, and without thinking it through, you uttered it, but now you regret it! Now you can go and make this sacrifice for having to recant it - the law here prescribes whether it is a lamb or a goat, or two doves or pigeons, and how it should be offered, etc. but these are no longer concerns for us in the new dispensation of grace, praise God!

One thing to note here is the belief that uttering such oaths were truly binding. This came from a Hebrew belief that 'words have power'. The basis of the modern 'Word of Faith' movement comes from that. However, whereas the Hebrew concept was that they had terrible power that we were to be aware of, and treat cautiously, the 'new idea' (though of course, it's not that new!) views the power within words as something to be harnessed - 'just speak what you want and it shall come to pass' is the mantra. While the Hebrew concept leads us to be careful with our tongue and warns us of the dangers of rash words and ill-thought statements and promises, the idea that we can speak things into happening through faith actually relies on us as mortal beings knowing what is good and right for us, but we do well to recall how we are flawed in discerning good and evil! Consider how the prodigal son thought he knew what was best for him as he left his father's house; only when he threw himself into his loving father's arms did he find real blessing. This is one reason I have the greatest disdain for such 'teaching' about prosperity; if we are careful about uttering what we want to, we shall not fall into the rash idea that we can have whatever we like. This caution causes us to actually have **more** faith in God because we are more able to accept that his own provision in our lives is better than what we ourselves think that we need. Again, since we need to note context every time we use scripture, this applies to the oft-quoted verse; *whatever you ask for in prayer, believe that you have received it, and it will be yours* (Mark 11:24) - Jesus had arrived in Jerusalem, had cleared the temple courts of the moneychangers, and cursed the barren fig-tree, so he was talking about being endowed with the power and authority that his disciples would need to go out and preach the kingdom message. No mention there of a brand new car... sorry, chariot! If you truly have a need of a car, God will provide it, so you don't need to name the one you'd like. We can also note from that amazing parable how the father actually gave in to his son's pleas for his inheritance! Even though he knew that it could well be bad for his son, he granted his wish. A loving father gives his children freewill, whatever the consequences might be! How much of what we heap upon ourselves as burdens (like financial debt, for example) are only due to our begging for things like a spoilt child! I say 'like' a spoilt child since I do not believe that our heavenly Father would ever spoil us, but the difference between the natural and the spiritual is that **we** can choose how much parenting God gives us - he shows us the example in the parable that he is a good enough Father to give us that freewill; we can choose to ignore his instruction and do our own thing, each and every moment. If we go after things that may not be beneficial for us, and we have a truly prodigal Father (prodigal means 'reckless' or impulsive, which the Father certainly was), are we capable of 'enticing' him to help us, or even to just allow us, to gain these things. There may, however, be another thing going on here, but it is controversial; Watchman Nee describes it in his book 'The Latent Power of the Soul' so I'll not elaborate on it.

Just as Jesus has already warned us about thoughts that lead us into sin, so we all can have a rashness in our minds that carelessly takes us into such a place of error regarding oaths. However, Jesus again is going beyond this simple provision, and while calling up what was 'said to the people long ago' that they should be careful to never break any oath but to fulfil it 'to the LORD' as they promised, he then does not simply offer this same provision... "but if it was made rashly, then here's how you can get out of it". No! He simply says "*do not swear an oath at all*" and states not to do it by **any** name or thing, neither in Earth nor Heaven. Unequivocally, he is calling a halt to such things. Why go further? In the law, we have an admission that sometimes oaths are not thought through properly and can be reversed, which is an allowance for the sin in our own hearts. Jesus, though, yet again, proclaims a 'higher' standard, that we are not to even bother making any such oaths; they should **not** trip off our tongue so lightly, but we should stop ourselves before such things are ever uttered and cease from it. What this achieves is a true 'change of heart' where the practicer of this command is more aware of their words and more able to not get caught in such traps. James the apostle warns us of this in his letter:

> "*We all stumble in many ways. Anyone who is never at fault in what they say is perfect, able to keep their*

whole body in check. When we put bits into the mouths of horses to make them obey us, we can turn the whole animal. Or take ships as an example. Although they are so large and are driven by strong winds, they are steered by a very small rudder wherever the pilot wants to go. Likewise, the tongue is a small part of the body, but it makes great boasts. Consider what a great forest is set on fire by a small spark. The tongue also is a fire, a world of evil among the parts of the body. It corrupts the whole body, sets the whole course of one's life on fire, and is itself set on fire by hell." (James 3:2-6)

So the provision this gives us is most certainly a help in the exercise of this very difficult control; may we all be able to maintain it more often than not, admitting that we will likely slip up on occasion, or maybe quite often! Jesus also addresses oaths in Matt. 23, in a great discourse against the religious teachers of his day:

"Woe to you, blind guides! You say, 'If anyone swears by the temple, it means nothing; but anyone who swears by the gold of the temple is bound by that oath.' You blind fools! Which is greater: the gold, or the temple that makes the gold sacred? You also say, 'If anyone swears by the altar, it means nothing; but anyone who swears by the gift on the altar is bound by that oath.' You blind men! Which is greater: the gift, or the altar that makes the gift sacred? Therefore, anyone who swears by the altar swears by it and by everything on it. And anyone who swears by the temple swears by it and by the one who dwells in it. And anyone who swears by

heaven swears by God's throne and by the one who sits on it." (16-22)

Here is a case of additional conditions being placed on what constitutes an oath and what doesn't, but Jesus decries this with clear language - **all** things one swears by count, and since he has already laid down the principle that we should **not** make oaths, then there are again no exceptions: one cannot follow this nonsensical teaching and negate any oath made depending on **what** it was sworn by! He's not trying to argue that some things are more or less 'powerful' or binding for swearing on; he's again decrying **any** swearing.

Added to this is the simple admonition to let our 'yes' be 'yes' and our 'no' be 'no' that our Lord tags on at the end, so if we are always being truthful, not given to lies, then we do not need to make any such swearing on anything! I remember when I was a young child in primary school, someone would ask me a question, or ask me to do something for them, and I'd answer them only to be challenged: "Do you swear? On your mother's life?" I never understood why I had to go through the ritual of holding my right hand up in the air while crossing my heart with my left hand and saying "I cross my heart, and hope to die, I swear to God, if I tell a lie!" and make such an oath on my mother's life, or my granny's grave, or... whatever it was that invoked such 'truth-telling'! I knew that I meant what I said, so I was affronted that I had to be demeaned in such a way and be doubted. Though I did know that many others were known to be liars and untrustworthy, and so those who had been lied to were just being prudent. And therein lies the lesson for us: Jesus wishes us to be truthful

at all times. We must not be like the father of lies, the devil (John 8:44), but like our Father in heaven, in whom is no falsehood, and indeed like the Son, in whom is no sin (1Jn. 3:5). We are exhorted to distinguish between the spirit of truth and the spirit of falsehood (1Jn. 4:6) and it only stands to reason that lying must not be a characteristic we are known for, nor must lying reside in any part of our character. Some may be more given to lying in their former nature - the old has gone, as Paul tells us (2Cor. 5:17), but it can still surface from time to time. The believer who can be found to be always truthful and therefore trustworthy must surely be in a better standing with others and have a better testimony for Christ! Can anyone refute this?

Unfortunately, in this era of social media, I far too often find fellow believers spreading untruths for their own ends (usually political), and even more worryingly, ignore any attempt to point out that what they have shared is false. 'The end justifies the means' should **not** be our mantra to excuse lies! If we cannot be wholly truthful in all our dealings for the kingdom, then we are **not** true ambassadors for it. Our king should be dismissing you from your role!

Therefore let us start by switching our mindset to one that knows that we do not have to swear any oaths to anyone, since our word is simply our bond. Let others know that you mean what you say and will do what you said. If your tongue does manage to get ahead of your brain and make such a rash promise that it needs to be recanted in order to make a better outcome than keeping the promise, then you can still repent of it, as is allowed, not from the law we discussed, but the applicable law of grace and continual forgiveness. We just need to make the best effort to not fall into such traps that we set for ourselves with this wrong mindset, but content ourselves that any slips into old ways are forgivable - no, they are forgiven! Praise God!! In taking this attitude, we perceive that this way Jesus shows us may be difficult, and may not always be adhered to, but it's certainly simpler! If you're not convinced, go and read the rest of that chapter in the Mosaic Law (Lev. 5) and see how complicated this was! Jesus' way may not be easier (though I hope we can find that it actually is!), but simpler. Therefore it is, in a way, easier; easier than all that having to travel to the Temple and do all that sacrificing.

An interesting point to note here is that while in the law, the literal blaspheming of the name of the Lord was punishable by death, there were other connotations to what blaspheming was. The name of course was YHWH, the blaspheming of which was so feared that it is even recorded as 'the Name'! It may be the equivalent of what we call 'taking his name in vain' since it was not to be used in uttering curses (e.g. Lev. 24:10-16), but the other connotation one finds in the OT is that his name is blasphemed by other people who see that the Lord's people have been removed from their land and are not being blessed by the Lord (e.g. Is. 52; Ez. 36). Why? When they turned from following his law and obeying him, they forfeited his promises (almost all covenants and promises made by God throughout scripture entertain conditions upon us) and lost his blessing and protection, and so when they were conquered or exiled, other peoples began to 'blaspheme' the name of the Lord by saying that he was not so great or he would have defended his people. He is a faithful God, which means he is also faithful to his promises, and so the forsaking of their part in such promises meant he could not act beyond its remits, and they then suffered the consequences of their actions - a result of their own infidelity to him. Paul expands on this (Rom. 2:17-29) by calling on those who call themselves lawkeeping Jews to ensure they then **do** keep the law, or they will invite others to blaspheme his name. Can we apply this to ourselves? Have you ever heard a non-believer say "well, he **calls** himself a Christian, but…"? By not living according to a decent moral standard, we invite others to blaspheme our Lord! Though a Christian should never be making such statements about another brother or sister - remember what we were discussing about judging!

For me, I wonder how I would react to being made to place my hand on a Bible and swear a testimony in court. Until that day happens, I'm not sure, but I am sure it would be ironic to state to the judge, "Sorry, but I cannot do that. I'm a Christian." However, what Jesus has commanded us is in many ways so much more radical than what is accepted as 'normal' Christian behaviour; this is just the beginning…

Eye for Eye

You have heard that it was said, 'Eye for eye, and tooth for tooth.' But I tell you, do not resist an evil person. If anyone slaps you on the right cheek, turn to them the other cheek also. And if anyone wants to sue you and take your shirt, hand over your coat as well. If anyone forces you to go one mile, go with them two miles. Give to the one who asks you, and do not turn away from the one who wants to borrow from you.

We now arrive at what may well be the most difficult of Jesus' commands! The dreaded 'turn the other cheek'! Is it dreaded? For sure, who of us likes it? Does it not go against every natural human urge we have, which tells us we must defend ourselves against attacks? Does this mean only physical assault? Only one kind of assault? More than just physical attacks? Once we investigate what Jesus meant, we shall see that it was a specific kind of assault he was referring to, but with the addition of the 'shirt and coat' and the 'extra mile' analogies, we can expand that to apply the principle to almost anything that is directed against us.

I have read much about these statements referring to the laws under Roman occupation. You may have heard them yourself. I managed to find confirmation of these claims on the striking of the cheek and the being forced to walk a mile. The latter one is found in an example from the region of Galatia, so it would have very likely been an edict cross the Empire. I shall leave the 'shirt and coat' to the end since it is slightly different.

Striking the cheek

In ancient cultures, especially where washing was not as easy or as commonplace as we have now, the right hand was used for greeting, eating and writing. The left was used for other purposes, particularly toileting. It was the 'unclean' hand and to greet someone with the left hand was insulting. Hence why children who were naturally left-handed were forced to write with their right hand. There was even a Bible printed for an Asian culture that had a misprint of a picture of Jesus raising his left hand in greeting. It had to be reprinted because it was so insulting. The latin for left is actually 'sinister'!

Slapping someone on the cheek was not the same as an all-out assault or picking a fight. The right hand was used, never the left, and the open hand was for equals in a challenge to them, maybe to a duel. This also occurred in more recent times, up to a few centuries ago, when often a glove was used. The back of the hand was for slaves and subordinates. Note how the phrasing Jesus uses is '*the right cheek*' - only a few English translations miss this word, and it's important when you consider it; the right hand being used to administer the slap would hit you on the **right** cheek if you were subordinate to the person slapping you. Then the slap was a reprimand and/or punishment for something. Turning the left cheek was a way of challenging **them** to treat you as an equal without retaliating. This was a case of 'passive resistance' to despotic authority, and his listeners would have recognised he was referring especially to the Romans. They were not to resist their overlords but they were to challenge them to treat them with more respect. It was a dignified response, even if an unusual one. Whether Romans actually understood the point being made is hard to gauge, though such behaviour would make them think, certainly.

Walking two miles

There was also this edict (or command issued) that a Roman soldier could press any citizen or subject of Rome to carry their heavy pack for them when they were travelling to or from their battalion, but there was a limit of one mile, so they couldn't force a person to go too far from their location or be pushed too much. This command from Jesus was another peculiar one that would be recognised in its reference to Rome. In this instance, the walking of one mile was not enough for our Lord. He wanted his followers to go that extra mile, and one would imagine that the soldier experiencing this would be confused; why would this subject go beyond what was asked of them? Might they be impressed by the compliance (and a cheerful compliance if one was doing it in service to God)? It has been suggested that doing this might place the soldier in trouble if it was thought that they had not stopped the carrier after the prescribed mile. If so, this would imply that this was the motive behind it. That's going beyond the text, and it's a valid way of reading it. To not go beyond the text would be narrowly pedantic, while being able to see past exactly what Jesus said would be to see the 'spirit' in which it was meant. The question for us, which is not easy to answer, is whether these teachings are meant to be clever insurrection against injustice, or simply a directive to go further than anyone else asks of you. It might be a better answer to conclude that there are elements of both motives. Think about the soldier, confronted by his superior who accuses him of making the poor carrier go beyond the one mile, and he pleads that the decision was made by the carrier to go further… is the carrier to not confirm that? To not do so would be to lie, and by admitting they really did choose to go further, they would surprise the soldier **and** their superior. Maybe the 'shirt and coat' example will shed light on this…

The shirt off your back, and the coat too

This case is different because Jesus is talking about being taken to court, not being 'oppressed' by the Romans. However, much of the social unrest in Judaea was due to the consequences of the Empire. The richest were taxing their subjects; the local rulers and landed people, and these people were passing on the burden to the poorest in further taxes and indebtedness. So the existence of this phenomenon today is yet again 'nothing new [under the sun]'. Someone being sued for 'the shirt off their back' would be at the lowest point, surely, with nothing left to give to pay their debt. In this case, the strange thing is Jesus saying that they should give their coat as well. The thing to note here is that a coat was used for sleeping in. I thought this must mean when travelling out in the open, but it was standard to do so. In Deuteronomy, there is a command concerning this very occurrence; someone who has made a loan to a neighbour may require a pledge, or a guarantee. They are not to enter the debtor's house but to wait for them to bring out the pledge. It would seem that this was usually the coat/ cloak (which is repeated in the chapter), but the lender is not to keep that pledge overnight:

> *If the neighbour is poor, do not go to sleep with their pledge in your possession. Return their cloak by sunset so that your neighbour may sleep in it. Then they will thank you, and it will be regarded as a righteous act in the sight of the Lord your God.* (Deut. 24:12,13)

So the argument could be made in this case that by handing over your coat to the debtor, you are shaming them, in front of the court, by suggesting that they will have gone too far if they take it. Any court at that time would refer the lender to that law and instruct them to **not** hold onto the coat. Is this really what Jesus is suggesting? I think we can see that the real difficulty here is determining the motive in Jesus' words. If you wish to view these commands as ways to resist oppression, then you could well see that being the driving force behind them. If you only want to see a policy of individuals offering themselves to others completely in an act of love, you will see this as what Jesus is saying. I have been concluding the latter for myself, but there truly is also the other aspect there; if you are set on a course of social action to defy what you believe is unjust and tyrannical, then this sort of passive action that offers more to the authorities would seem to be the best way, and it fits into the ethos of universal love that we shall see unfold here.

My argument is that all these commands taken together (on top of these three) do not appear to have any sort of ulterior motive beyond the message of love. From **that** standpoint, all else will follow anyway. My problem with the 'passive social action' argument is that it tends to take these three small commands in isolation, and it feels to me like the reason (or motive) for doing these things is to 'wipe their eye' or to get one over on those who would take from you, yet both before and after these three, they are qualified. The 'you have heard…' here is "Eye for eye, tooth for tooth" and it must be noted that this is repeated in the Mosaic law as a **restriction** and not a blanket allowance for revenge and retribution. The basic principle is that if someone takes your eye, you can't take their leg, metaphorically, and you are limited to demanding only what would be just recompense for your loss. The 'evil person' that Jesus refers to is clearly the one who would deliberately take your eye or your tooth, and he is going beyond this restriction that prevents you taking too much back, and telling us to *not resist* the evil person. This is a general command which has nothing to do with social resistance. This is also upheld by the last verse in this section; *Give to the one who asks you, and do not turn away from the one who wants to borrow from you.* This goes further still! Anyone who 'asks you' for something, or wishes to borrow from you is obviously not necessarily an 'evil person' - many of our good friends and relatives may ask us for things or seek to borrow from us. Since Jesus makes it clear here that we must not *turn away from the one who wants to borrow* from us, this is certainly about more than social resistance. Luke's account of this sermon even includes his instruction: *lend to them without expecting to get anything back.* In other words, give; if it comes back, great. If not, don't sweat. Can we really do that in our human limitations?

I see the value of applying this to social resistance, and the lesson there is good. My problem with it is that many use that as a chance to dismiss these commands and say that we're taking them out of context. While I have pointed out the importance of context, it's not a get-out clause; examine the whole thing in the light of what is said before and after it, and you can see how it has a broader application. There are portions of scripture that even the most ardent inerrantist will relegate to history and proclaim as having no application to today, but this isn't one of them, nor does it only apply to Christians facing persecution. It is the principles that persecuted believers can use, therefore they become tools of peaceful resistance. Add to that; if being taken to court for not baking a particular cake for a thorny customer is 'persecution', then how would we apply these principles? Have these principles actually been applied in such cases? What do you think would be the outcome if they were? We could even go back to the clear command from v.25: *Settle matters quickly with your adversary who is taking you to court.*

To ensure that any of this confusion is laid aside, and in case any of the hearers are going through the thoughts of 'this can't be right' and 'surely he doesn't mean what I think he means?', which I am pretty sure many of them were, Jesus delivers the last of his 'you have heard that it was said' monologues, and it's the biggest of them all!...

Love your enemies

> *You have heard that it was said, 'Love your neighbour and hate your enemy.' But I tell you, love your enemies and pray for those who persecute you, that you may be children of your Father in heaven. He causes his sun to rise on the evil and the good, and sends rain on the righteous and the unrighteous. If you love those who love you, what reward will you get? Are not even the tax collectors doing that? And if you greet only your own people, what are you doing more than others? Do not even pagans do that? Be perfect, therefore, as your heavenly Father is perfect.*

Jesus **knows** that he has to take us one more step beyond merely not taking an eye for an eye. The idea that we are never to seek vengeance or recompense for wrongs done to us may be radical enough, but at his no 'eye for an eye' command, he had already gone beyond the mere passivity of **not** wanting such repayments from anyone to making it an **active** thing: he already told his followers to go further if asked to do something. In that last command, we were not just to turn the other cheek, but were to offer **more** - if sued for a shirt, to give our coat as well, and if asked to go one mile, to go two miles! Earlier I dealt with our personal anger and how it is vital to overcome it, but left out the point Jesus was making to us to be **active** in how we deal with enemies (overcoming anger is not just about us); I left that until now because it ties in with this last one perfectly, since simply **being** generous with them is a command, but it does **not** go far enough.

No, just as he views our harbouring of evil thoughts in our heads as examples of murder and adultery, so here too the **act** of giving to an enemy must be bolstered by a change of heart! Right away, just as the previous shocking command to seek no wrong for wrong but to give willingly to an enemy is sinking in, he says that we are to **love** our enemies! And to pray for those who **persecute** us! Persecutors!? Really? Pray **for** them? Yes!! And just in case some in the crowd were saying "well, yes, if I'm fit enough and can carry that soldier's pack for two miles, I've saved a fellow Israelite from the same fate!" Jesus makes it **absolutely clear** that loving your own is no better than the tax collectors (selfish traitors who extorted money for the Roman oppressors **and** themselves, in the eyes of the Jews) or the pagans (unbelievers who worship false gods!). His standard **is** indeed higher, and he even suggests that this 'loving of enemies' is required in order that we '*may be children of [our] Father in heaven.*' He had already said earlier in his sermon that the peacemakers were blessed *"for they will be called children of God"* (5:9): was he not then saying that those of us who do **not** make peace with our enemies will **not** be called God's children? Can we simply infer the converse? In simpler terms, if I say, for example, that I only wear T-shirts, then could you take from that if someone found a buttoned shirt in my church that it could not be mine, since it was **not** a T-shirt? Can we then make such an inference from Jesus' words here? That those who do **not** make peace or love their enemies **cannot** be called children of God? Many might argue against this and say it is taking the words and message of Jesus too far, but that attitude could also imply that his words are not to be taken too seriously. **That** is a dangerous place to find oneself, is it not?

What if my proposal is wrong, and we may **not** infer a converse meaning from this, and these things are **not** important to our status as 'children of God'? How does this affect our 'salvation' and our relationship with Christ? For now, let us just consider the implication of this belief - we are then saying that a direct command of our Lord becomes unimportant. This is a very different thing to saying it is 'secondary' or 'additional' - saying it is **unimportant** removes it from having any place in our lives and we can choose whether to do it or not; it is **this** sort of thinking that the licensers seem to revel in - that since our salvation is achieved once for all time by Jesus and that is achieved for us individually at the moment we accept that salvation, then we have no need for such commands. They are there for those who want to think they are important, but you can ignore them if you so desire, since 'you're saved anyway'! If you truly believe that salvation is not achieved by works, then you can come down clearly on the side of the argument that commands like 'love your enemies' are **not** important. However, ask me: is it important for salvation? No, not salvation. However, I will ask you: not important at all? If you answer 'no', then why do you seriously call yourself a Christian or a follower of Jesus? What did Jesus say about that?

> *If you love me, keep my commands... Whoever has my commands and keeps them is the one who loves me.* (John 14:15, 21)

Now we do know that our salvation is finished on the cross at Calvary. The writer to the Hebrews knew this and proclaimed it:

> *Day after day every priest stands and performs his religious duties; again and again he offers the same sacrifices, which can never take away sins. But when this priest had offered for all time one sacrifice for sins, he sat down at the right hand of God, and since that time he waits for his enemies to be made his footstool. For by one sacrifice he has made perfect forever those who are being made holy.*
>
> *The Holy Spirit also testifies to us about this. First he says:*
> > *"This is the covenant I will make with them after that time, says the Lord.*
> > *I will put my laws in their hearts, and I will write them on their minds."*
> *Then he adds:*

"Their sins and lawless acts
I will remember no more."

And where these have been forgiven, sacrifice for
sin is no longer necessary. (Heb. 7:11-18)

The writer here clearly nails his theology to the post for all
to see! Quoting from Jeremiah (31:33-34), he talks of a
foretold time that would come when the *'sins and lawless*
acts' of some, he would *'remember no more'* and this time
has come since *"this priest* [has already] *offered for all time*
one sacrifice for sins" and has *'sat down'* to rest at the
completion of his work. This Jesus has done it all! Proclaim
it! But note what else he quoted from Jeremiah: *"I will put*
my laws in their hearts" - is this not what we have been
reading right through this sermon? In his sermon, Jesus is
telling his followers to follow a law within their hearts, that
constrains them to be obedient to his teaching, this 'higher
standard' we have discovered, that is so much more than a
rule book to which we turn as if we were in a courtroom
and seek approval from a judge that the letter of the law has
been kept. Did Jesus not make this clear to the Pharisees
about divorce, just for one example? No, we **are** the people
foretold by Jeremiah, the ones for whom our sins will no
longer be remembered, but also those who have his law
written on our hearts!

And he also states *"he has made perfect forever those who*
are being made holy" - we who have been made (done,
completed, finished) 'perfect forever' are also (presently,
currently) 'being made holy'!! Recall the laying out and
distinction between justification and sanctification: Our
perfection is something established in God's eyes already

by Calvary's cross, and this is both mysterious and scandalous to us - remember that we are **deemed** holy, **but** our present walk with Christ in this world is a work in progress. **The pursuit of holiness is an ongoing thing, despite our permanent perfection in Christ**. 1Peter reinforces this with saying that we have been *"chosen… to be **obedient** to Jesus Christ **and** sprinkled with his blood."* (1Pet. 1:2, emphasis mine) - so God wants us to be both saved by Christ's blood and obedient to Jesus at the same time! I'll not venture into my view of the nature of predestination here; you can find that in my blogs!

So here in this last command of this series, he states that if we do **not** love our enemies, we may **not** be children of our Father in heaven? No? His earlier beatitudes of *"Blessed are the…"* form (5:3-12) can be taken as commands too. Warren Wiersbe wrote a series of 27 commentaries across the OT, known as the 'Be series' with titles such as 'Be strong', 'Be holy', 'Be obedient', Be comforted', etc. These served to show me that most theology can be turned around into an active form of command and instruction for us as believers. For me, theology that isn't practical may be interesting at times, but it is of little value. If you simply turn these statements into a negative, is it not clear that they are indeed commands? - "Those who do not make peace will **not** be blessed!"? He is not simply **stating** that peacemakers will be called children of God (or just **stating** that if we love our enemies, we might also be accredited this title). No, these are commands from him in how we act and think - we are to **be** meek, pure in heart, merciful, and to hunger and thirst for righteousness. How else would we expect to be blessed? We cannot just ask for blessing, we must strive to **be** the very people he describes, then we **will** be blessed, just as he proclaims! So also, we must take these difficult commands seriously and seek to obey them as best as we can, including finding a **love** for enemies. This is not a cosy feeling nor an order to 'be nice to them' - not if it comes from an unloving heart, and is done grudgingly or unwillingly. No, the command here is *agapao*, the verbal form of *agapē*, which is the unconditional love that is all-conquering, that Jesus showed in his death for us on the cross. If we are to ask the question "why are so many marriages failing these days?", one simple answer could be that we have a generation that seek what **feels** good, not what **is** good - the lovey-dovey gooey feeling you get with your new love as a youngster does not last long into a marriage where you are living together day in, day out. True love is **not** that feeling (which in Greek is *eros*, from which we get 'erotic love'; *eros* never occurs in the NT)! The command for husbands to love their wives (Eph. 5:25; Col. 3:19) is *agapao*!). It is an action, a pursuit, a striving to be more like him, a determined desire to show and express love, maybe even to the point of death (John 15:13), to **everyone**, friend and foe alike, universally, unequivocally; John ties these obedience of commands to love in a perfect loop:

> *And this is love: that we walk in obedience to his commands. As you have heard from the beginning, his command is that you walk in love.* (2John 1:6)

The original Greek only records love (*agapē*) once in this verse; the last instance of 'love' in the NIV is actually *autē* which is referencing back to the original, and simply translated in other versions as 'it' - the NIV is just establishing in case there is any doubt: the 'it' references what John is addressing here - 'love'. Not all languages have an equivalent of English 'it' and the Greek *autē* is similar but not used in exactly the same way, so placing 'love' there by the NIV is perfectly correct in linguistic terms. John's second letter, to a beloved sister in Christ, is a short greeting and is chiefly just a confirmation of the original command to love! John defines love as walking in his commands, and his command is that we walk in love. How do we know we are walking in love? We are obedient to his commands! We could just go in endless, glorious circles here - let your head spin in awe at this!

If you're still wondering about this, or fighting this in your head, conscious that none of these commands have any bearing on our stand with God, our 'salvation in Christ' or our entrance into the Kingdom, then there's a real problem, and I don't know how else to get you around that. Do you not **want** to obey Jesus? Consider this:

> *God does not need your good works, but your neighbour does!*
>
> - Martin Luther

Also this: one Sunday in church, a friend's son came to us and told us that our seven-year old granddaughter had pushed him over. We called her to ask why. Apparently he was annoying her. We told her that was no excuse for pushing him, and told her to apologise to him. She didn't want to, but in the end she did, because we demanded it. As she walked away, at the door, I heard her mutter under her breath: "I'd push him again!" I couldn't help but laugh, but I realised that her apology was empty. It was only for us, not him, nor even herself. She had no desire in her heart to be sorry. If we only show love to others and do as they bid us in response to the demands of Jesus, without wishing in our own hearts to do so, is that not just empty too? There are many things of God which we don't understand, and we can turn to the old oft-repeated quote that 'his ways are not our ways', but that is one verse that is taken out of context too often! The whole thing about quoting "my ways are not your ways" is, as it **always** is, to place it in context. It's from Isaiah's prophecies; chapter 55. Read that chapter, and put it directly in the middle where it belongs, because that proclamation is solely about reconciliation, forgiveness, restoration of all the nations, even nations 'not known' by Israel, and the 'everlasting covenant of love' he has established... '**This** will be the Lord's renown... that will endure forever.' We might be the ones who want vengeance or justice on our enemies, but the Lord is **way** beyond that in our thinking. It is a glorious chapter to read!

As we come to the end of these '*But I tell you...*' commands, we must recognise just how serious they are! We cannot write them off, explain them away, skirt around them, or decide they're not relevant for us, or do not apply in the 21st century, or anything else like that. If we take our scripture seriously as a manual for Christian living, then surely Jesus' direct commands to us are the most important and unbendable of these scripture verses? We all do our fair share of rethinking verses or contextualising them, **all** of us, without exception, but bad treatment of the commands of this sermon must run us into the greatest danger, yes?

> *"To fail to love like Jesus is the worst form of heresy, regardless of how true one's beliefs are."*
> - Greg Boyd

Conclusion: so WHAT does he say to us?

So can we now find a definition for sin? As discussed, the label of 'disobedience to God' does not cover everything since we may disagree on some of these things that we may or may not view as disobedient. I can hear the dissenting cry of "That's moral relativism!" - it may well be, if you wish to give it that label, and disrespect it as a 'worldly' attitude that ignores the law of God, but I refer you to the 14th chapter of Paul's letter to the Romans; it's too involved to go into here, but Paul clearly states that one thing, like maintaining a single day as holy, may be a very righteous thing for one follower but mean nothing to another, and neither is to disrespect or judge the other.

If we can arrive at a basic conclusion that what Jesus was addressing in his sermon is everything to do with how we think **and** how we treat others, and the links that exist between internal attitudes and thoughts, and external behaviour. In order to be better followers of his example of unconditional and sacrificial love, we first must strive to rectify bad things within us that may undermine what efforts we make to 'live better lives'. If we allow selfish, self-gratifying thoughts about the opposite sex to go unhindered in our minds, we may end up seeing them in a wrong light and approach a relationship with what we can **get** from it rather than how we can engage with the fellow human being or how we can truly love the person and enhance **their** life. If we make no attempt to curb feelings of anger within ourselves, even if the anger has been justified, we may also begin to engage with individuals aggressively (although maybe often unwittingly - have you never been in a situation where someone you are talking to has asked you to calm down and you have been unaware that you actually were behaving this way?). Not having an attitude of love at all times may lead us into sin. Jesus taught us to love even our enemies, so each living breathing individual on this planet, regardless of whatever wrong they may have done, is deserving of our love. I will not water down what my Lord said about this in any way! People who have been evil or have done wrong will be subject to the laws of their own country and also ultimately stand before the all-knowing throne of The Judge, but we are not to judge these people and dismiss them as unworthy. If I truly believe that Jesus died for all mankind, then he died for **all** mankind - there is not one person for whom the offer of his grace is not to be shown or extended. We must preach the gospel of Jesus and witness for his grace to **everyone**, without any personal favour or bias. If we truly believe he can forgive sin, then that means **all** sin, no matter how bad or disgusting we may think it is! Since he is the final arbiter of who has accepted God's grace, I must defer to God alone on that. Such anger that we may feel **can** affect our witness and testimony, as I well know. Not so long ago, I allowed a hatred of a particular political philosophy lead me into error. I believe it (free market ideology) is the cause of most of our 21st century problems, and have traced it back to an early heresy (religious dualism, and particularly Marcionism), but I projected that hatred onto one political figure in particular, and ended up posting a really vile meme on social media about her. She is an individual (rather, was, since she has already left this world), loved by God, as I have stated, and I too must not allow myself to fall into hatred of the **person**, while maintaining my anger over what I see as unjust and evil in this world. I had to write a blog about the plank in **my** own eye and eat humble pie! Too often we allow a distaste for certain political or religious beliefs or doctrines to lead us into a solid disdain for the proponents of that idea, and this can cause hatred of individuals - let us each keep watch on this problem! Note that my statement about God loving every human being is **not** an endorsement of the theology that every person will be saved, regardless of religious belief or acceptance of the grace of God through Christ! Often too, when certain things you read in a book **sound** like the same things that somebody else has been saying, it is too easy to 'tar that with the same brush' and dismiss it. Even easier to decide, from one point of doctrine you disagree with or one foolish remark over something you hold precious, to remove all influence and writings of a thinker or theologian from your life. This is presumptive, and has become a modern phenomenon among social media known as 'cancel culture'. May we be able to be more accepting (**and** discerning) towards those with whom we hold different doctrines and beliefs, instead of having the usual human knee-jerk reactions to them.

I think we can also safely conclude that this following Jesus stuff is not easy! Many forms of religious Christianity simply pay lip service to ritual and church attendance with little thought on anything else that Jesus might have been asking us to do all along. We can fall into a 'comfort zone' of following after a creed or a 'way of life' that we set up as necessary to show the world that we are Christians when in fact we may be ignoring the very virtues and attributes that he himself has called us to display! I recall in a church I attended as a young man, the pastor said that if someone saw you walking up the street on a Sunday morning in your

'Sunday best' with a bible under your arm, they knew you were a Christian: I remarked to myself that I only knew they were a churchgoer!

If this is indeed very difficult (and by the admission that he is perfect and we are not we must concede that we will certainly **not** be able to attain his example consistently), then just **how** do we even get started on this journey? Such an admission can lead us quickly into a very poor fatalist-type attitude that we may not really achieve anything **like** a sin-free life, so why try? This, I fear, is a starting point for many licensers - they've just decided to give up trying! If you are like me in seeking to follow he who is the Way properly, and commit to it, you'll want a **genuine** experience, not one resigned to failure, nor one that will always be fleeing from us as quickly as we catch up on it. So accepting that we will not be perfect on this earth is the first position - from here we can have a healthy and balanced view of how we are compared to how we should be. If we cannot attain perfection, then surely **any** movement along this path must be good? Yes? How much we 'improve' or how far we go with Jesus is an individual thing and each of us will be accountable for our progress over the years of our life. A good classic to read is John Bunyan's 'The Pilgrim's Progress', which likens the trials of the believer to a journey with various metaphors relating to the things we all face.

In all that he taught about the cost of following him, however difficult it was, would you not believe that a loving Lord like him would give us proper advice on how we are to be more fully able to follow him? Why would he make commands for us that would be so difficult as to discourage us and lead us to excuse them away? When the disciples witnessed his interaction with the rich young man, they were amazed at his statement to the man to give up all his wealth before following him, and then his claim about putting a camel through the eye of the needle being easier than a rich person entering heaven; they wondered 'who then can be saved?' His answer to them was *"With man this is impossible, but with God all things are possible."* (Matt. 19:26). Here we have the basis of how we achieve these things that are seemingly impossible, from this context, his provision for us! If we have grasped the concept of how we are saved by grace, through no effort from us, then the following is surely also achieved by the same means?

He has laid down for us some simple principles that can be summed up as 'change of heart'. They are simple to comprehend and seek to follow, but they are **not** easy. They don't have all the complexities of the Mosaic Law, which Jesus summed up as two commands:

> *Jesus replied: '"Love the Lord your God with all your heart and with all your soul and with all your mind." This is the first and greatest commandment. And the second is like it: "Love your neighbour as yourself." All the Law and the Prophets hang on these two commandments.'* (Matt. 22: 37-40)

Love comes from the heart, the seat of our emotions, and so this shows how and where 'heart change' occurs; the application of love. The law of Christ which Paul referred to is just this; what we have just read! Simple commands to change our heart, and to apply love to everything we do, but (and this is part of the wonder of it all) he is the one leading in front of us and we only need to step in his footprints! "How can I match up to the example of the Son of God?" I may hear you protest. He told us clearly that *whoever believes in me will do the works I have been doing, and they will do even greater things than these, because I am going to the Father* (John 14:12). Therefore we **will** be able to do these things; the 'works' that he did are far more than just the miracles. He was establishing his kingdom of love, grace and forgiveness. Restoring the Kingdom of Restoration. So we can and will do the same, and take his kingdom further (more). Just how he offers help, and makes even simpler requests, will be seen in the next section. He certainly doesn't leave his audience hanging in this case; he reserved that tactic for those who were **not** of his flock. We can be assured that we are being instructed carefully and thoroughly. Simpler than the Law, and the Prophets, but not easier. Simple, not easy, but assisted all along. Praise his name!

Part 2: Be Humble

Give humbly

> *Be careful not to practise your righteousness in front of others to be seen by them. If you do, you will have no reward from your Father in heaven. 'So when you give to the needy, do not announce it with trumpets, as the hypocrites do in the synagogues and on the streets, to be honoured by others. Truly I tell you, they have received their reward in full. But when you give to the needy, do not let your left hand know what your right hand is doing, so that your giving may be in secret. Then your Father, who sees what is done in secret, will reward you.*

At this point in the sermon, we actually enter into a 'simpler' phase. Jesus has laid out some really, truly difficult commands to his followers but now he just points out how we are to be humble in all we do. The opening verse to this chapter makes a fairly clear statement that had somehow passed by me. I wonder if it passed you too? If we don't keep secret our 'giving' to the needy, we *will have no reward* from our Father! Seems a bit harsh, I thought. However, if you only give to others in order to receive some sort of reward or praise, then is it not clear that your motive is wrong? In analysing this, I have to apply it to myself. I don't have a lot of money on this Earth, so I could easily dismiss this as not applying to me, though whatever I give others from my means must be subject to this criterion. I recall how Jesus made it clear that the widow who gave two small coins was more generous than all the rich before her who put in plenty (Mark 12:41-43). Therefore whatever I give, however small an amount it is that I can manage, it must still also be secret, simply to comply with this command. I also realise that I must include time and effort, and not just money. These things are given by Jesus followers for various causes and needs (or they should!).

A problem that can arise has been given a name I have only heard recently: virtue signalling. This means that someone is trying to show others how much they care about an issue or about other people, and might even use it to bash those who don't. In other words, they trumpet their 'good works'. Cynically, I would try to point out that those who don't care about causes use this slur to demean those who do care. I believe there must be an element of this present, but if I fall into this trap of cynicism, I have failed already to remain humble, and can easily think of myself as 'better' (more highly than I ought) than the uncaring. Certainly, Jesus is not the uncaring and is not crying out against virtue signalling, so his command is valid. From my own experience, I can posit that at least one of the causes of virtue signalling comes from the judgement of others. In my own experience, the thought that others might look at my life and think that I am lazy, or useless in some way, can lead me to try to let people know about the good things that I do e.g. voluntary work, or the attempts I make to contribute to others with my (unrecognised) talents. I am always aware that I have not been a 'lifelong taxpaying worker'; I have had periods of having to look after my wife in periods of illness, a few times when I was a full-time student (including a period at Bible College when I had zero official income and truly 'lived by faith'), three times self-employed unsuccessfully (now four, hoping), and yes, a few full-time paid jobs. I can look back on it all with a clear conscience that I made the efforts, was committed and busy, but was a product of the circumstances. I'm tempted to use 'victim' but that is such a loaded word, it's inappropriate. Throughout everything, God has always, consistently, ever, provided for us, sometimes truly miraculously. I know in my heart that I can stand on that and declare the truth of it, so why do I actually become a victim of the judgements of others? Yes, that is a case where we become victims! In the same way that I must avoid judging others, they must also avoid judging me! Therefore, if they do make a judgement upon me, whether I am aware of it or not, that is entirely their problem, and **not mine**. If I think that they **are** judging me, then am I not also making a judgment about them? This may seem like a very circular problem, but if I get to the place where I no longer truly care if anyone else makes a judgement on me, then this all vanishes. Why would it not? I live my life as between me and God, and nobody else. This doesn't mean that I don't care about anybody else, because God calls me clearly to care about others. The selfish person lives only for themselves. The balanced Jesus follower lives only for Jesus. The following makes you into someone who cares about people, but doesn't care about what they think of you: only what Jesus thinks about me should be important to me. If I am a truly humble person, then I will fulfil those commands that I know Jesus has given me, and I then should become more like Jesus, and will draw love, warmth and praise from those who see it. I will also draw anger and misunderstanding from those who don't want to see The Way of Jesus. I must still love them all the same, just as I was commanded. Maybe they will be won over to also following Jesus by that.

Pray humbly

And when you pray, do not be like the hypocrites, for they love to pray standing in the synagogues and on the street corners to be seen by others. Truly I tell you, they have received their reward in full. But when you pray, go into your room, close the door and pray to your Father, who is unseen. Then your Father, who sees what is done in secret, will reward you. And when you pray, do not keep on babbling like pagans, for they think they will be heard because of their many words. Do not be like them, for your Father knows what you need before you ask him.

'This, then, is how you should pray:
'"Our Father in heaven,
hallowed be your name,
your kingdom come,
your will be done,
    on earth as it is in heaven.
Give us today our daily bread.
And forgive us our debts,
    as we also have forgiven our debtors.
And lead us not into temptation,
    but deliver us from the evil one."
For if you forgive other people when they sin against you, your heavenly Father will also forgive you. But if you do not forgive others their sins, your Father will not forgive your sins.

I hate prayer meetings! Those who know me now will probably do a right double take at that, since I'm hardly away from them! Let me explain: I was always the shy one. I hate squealing children, but I also hated them when I **was** a child. I would be the one with my hands over my ears at a screaming toddlers' party. This was also the case when I went to my grammar school and decided to join the debating society. I was terrible at public speaking, and could not really take part in the debates because I would get tongue-tied. I also had an 'impediment': I spoke too fast. I was very eloquent as a toddler, my mother always told me, so how I ended up being virtually unintelligible to others is a mystery. I only really overcame these problems and improved my public speaking abilities as a young adult at Bible college, and had to hone the skills over many years.

This was the problem with prayer meetings; they were more about how 'great' a prayer one could pray, using all the right words in the right order. I never understood why we had to say things like "we ask for journeying and travelling mercies" on everyone as they left a meeting! Things like that just put me off prayer meetings; it seemed as if you had to be 'properly trained' in praying, when we all know it's just talking to God. The best prayers for me were the heartfelt ones that somebody prayed who had no idea they were meant to use 'the jargon'. Is this not exactly what Jesus was condemning? *...do not keep on babbling like pagans, for they think they will be heard because of their many words.* Yet here we are, 2000 years later, falling into the same pattern. Nothing new under the sun! I could try to examine why this happens, but I would only end up judging those who do it, which is somewhere I shall choose to avoid. It is only up to me to not be like this. It's up to you too. The reason I find that I love prayer meetings now is twofold; firstly, I recognise the value and power of prayer. I have seen the results on too many occasions to dismiss it, and communal prayer is vital to add efficacy (power or effectiveness), and help the bonds of unity and fellowship, since we can 'pray together' as was done by the church (Acts 1:14) when the power of Pentecost fell upon them. Secondly, I have become far less retiring when speaking in public, but not that I have 'learnt the jargon'; I have purely become more confident in knowing that I can speak to God as I speak to any friend, and doing this in public is not that different. It is true that a prayer made in a meeting is also for others to hear, but the impression should be made upon God, not them. They should be joining in with the sentiment, not the rhetoric, with the feeling, not the words. God is not impressed by such words, as he has just told us! The best prayers are actually those done when we *go into [our] room* and *close the door*!

The Lord's Prayer is now recited as a magical effective prayer when it was simply an example from Jesus as to **how** we should pray. It is simple enough, and a template upon which we should base other prayers, but can we make it even simpler?

1. Our Father in heaven is holy.
2. May his kingdom come, not just in heaven but on Earth too.
3. Give us what we need today.
4. Forgive us; yes, we've forgiven others.
5. Keep us from evil. [The article is used for 'evil' in the Greek, so most translations render it 'the evil one']

Only a few things to note here. We might always pray for his kingdom to come, and for it to be evident around us, but what do we actually do to assist that? If we are obeying his commands in our lives, is that not extending the kingdom? To define the Kingdom of God; a kingdom is simply where a king is obeyed, where he can apply his laws. If the people rebel against his laws, he might lose that kingdom. So it is with God; if his will is being done, that is where his kingdom is. Jesus said that God's kingdom is in our midst, or within us (Luke 17:21), and that it is like mustard seeds that grow, or yeast that works through the dough (Matt. 13:31-33), so by our working it out, we can spread that seed, or knead the yeast through all the dough. The humble follower will know that whatever this entails, it is not beneath them.

We are not exhorted to pray for bread for the next year, nor to pray for a slow roast pulled beef sandwich with dill pickle, garlic mayo and Castelvetranos olives! While these things are delicious and to be enjoyed if/when we can, I have always thought it presumptive to pray beyond what we need. I have seen God supply our needs constantly, and also provide us with some nice luxuries too, but my prayer should only be for sustenance. He knows my heart, and knows what I like. He is the Good Father who will look after me, but the prayer said in humility will be satisfied with bread each day if that is all that comes along. The Israelites in the desert learnt that their manna was only to be collected each day and not to be hoarded for the next. Hoarding is so much the opposite of humility and trust, since God provides each and every day. Paul learnt to trust in God for each day and be content, even when facing shipwreck, flogging, prison and death!

It would be amiss to ignore the point that Jesus made after the prayer, since he was clearly emphasising: *if you do not forgive others their sins, your Father will not forgive your sins*. Following in humility will cause us to be much more willing to forgive, since we have already been warned about that plank. Jesus wants us to be plankless, in order to receive the forgiveness for our own sins and faults, that we eagerly desire. I have noticed, reading through the gospels, of how Jesus simply said to the man lowered on the mat, and the woman who washed his feet "your sins are forgiven" yet we know that the message of the gospel is 'repentance for the forgiveness of sins' (Luke 3:3; 24:47). I see the heart's desire of Jesus to forgive so readily, but if we are too proud to admit the plank needs removing, then we are the ones standing in the way of his love. Surely his love is the greatest and strongest force in the universe? And is God not love? Yes, but I don't believe it chooses to bash down our door and take our heart by force. It simply stands outside and knocks to gain entrance. We are the ones who need to open the door, and we do that through humility and recognising that we need to learn to love the way that he does, and so we open the door to the world to love and forgive those outside. Note that the door he is knocking to gain entrance in Rev. 3:20 is addressed to the church (at Laodicea), **not** unbelievers, as it is often misused!

> *Whoever does not love does not know God, because God is love.* (1John 4:8)

Fast humbly

> *When you fast, do not look sombre as the hypocrites do, for they disfigure their faces to show*

111

others they are fasting. Truly I tell you, they have received their reward in full. But when you fast, put oil on your head and wash your face, so that it will not be obvious to others that you are fasting, but only to your Father, who is unseen; and your Father, who sees what is done in secret, will reward you.

Fasting is a sacrament that has been largely forgotten in the modern church. Richard Foster deals with it also in 'Celebration of Discipline' and what it entails, means, and achieves for the believer. I shall leave the topic for him and other authors, or another time, maybe. The lesson here is that when fasting, like giving and prayer, we must do it humbly and secretly. For our purposes here, I believe Jesus is talking about the suffering we endure when fasting i.e. the hunger, or the loss of whatever it is that we are giving up for a period. Some traditions still have the practice of 'giving up something for Lent' to practice an experience similar to Jesus in the wilderness. Whichever way it is done, for whatever reason, any suffering we are enduring should not be apparent to others. We should not be a 'Moaning Minnie' and wear down those around us with our wails. Now I must mention a pet peeve I have always had; the perceived 'norm' that when someone greets us with "How are you?" We must always reply "Fine, thank you. How are you?" I have always valued friends that I knew wanted more than the platitude, and would not mind if I said something like "Oh, I still haven't got that appointment with the doctor, and this pain is getting worse!" and they could empathise and show genuine concern. That requires the closeness of a friend, or a true fellow brother or sister, who can help to shoulder that burden (and I can empathise with them when needed), but for the rest of humanity around us, this should not be something we display. A fair face, smiling at those around us, is a great thing to spread:

Smiling is infectious,
you catch it like the flu,
When someone smiled at me today,
I started smiling too.
I passed around the corner
and someone saw my grin.
When he smiled I realised
I'd passed it on to him.
I thought about that smile,
then I realised its worth.
A single smile, just like mine
could travel round the earth.
So, if you feel a smile begin,
don't leave it undetected.
Let's start an epidemic quick,
and get the world infected!

- Spike Milligan

Serve humbly

Do not store up for yourselves treasures on earth,
where moths and vermin destroy, and where thieves
break in and steal. But store up for yourselves
treasures in heaven, where moths and vermin do
not destroy, and where thieves do not break in and
steal. For where your treasure is, there your heart
will be also.

'The eye is the lamp of the body. If your eyes are
healthy, your whole body will be full of light. But if
your eyes are unhealthy, your whole body will be
full of darkness. If then the light within you is
darkness, how great is that darkness!
'No one can serve two masters. Either you will hate
the one and love the other, or you will be devoted to
the one and despise the other. You cannot serve
both God and Money.

A clear distinction between the nature of light and darkness.
However, what is Jesus really saying here? Treasures on
Earth, then 'healthy' eyes, then comparing serving God and
Money? Many have taken each on their own, as a list of
sayings, but there truly is a connection. I noticed a footnote
in the NIV that said the word 'unhealthy' can also mean
stingy. The word is *poneyros* in the Greek, which is usually
just 'evil' (as in the Lord's Prayer above), but this word can
have a number of meanings. One of them actually is to be
stingy and miserly. Further investigation uncovers that a
number of translations use 'if thine eye be evil/ if your eye
is evil' and this corresponds to one verse in the OT. The
expression 'evil eye' and that theme is found throughout
scripture, especially in older translations, but this particular
phrase is repeated in just this verse and Deut. 15:9. The
Greek LXX translation of the OT uses the same phrasing
that is found in this passage. I would really prefer to use
'evil' - the desire to contextualise the word to 'unhealthy'
here is usually what is required, but it forgets the reference
that I believe Jesus was pointing to. What is that exactly?
Deut. 15: 7-11 deals with what to do with a 'brother who
has become poor' and the command is to not turn away
from him (making your eye evil towards him *or* harbouring

a wicked thought) and ignore him, especially if you are approaching the 'the seventh year, the year of release' when all debts were cancelled (yes!), but one is to give ungrudgingly in order to be blessed by the Lord.

Therefore there is no disconnection here. We are to store up treasure in heaven instead of earth, for our eye must be healthy (not evil), or it will not let in the light and we shall be in darkness, and we must not serve both God and Money. We will love one and hate the other. This ties in with other scripture; as already mentioned, in Luke's version of Jesus commanding us to love our enemies, Jesus says *love your enemies, do good to them, and lend to them without expecting to get anything back* (6:35). John describes the love of the world while telling us to avoid it, and uses *the lust of the eyes* (1John 2:16) as one of the things which stands against loving the Father.

We store up treasure in heaven, not by simply being generous, but by doing all that we are asked to do by Christ. All that we have read in this sermon, and all we are still to read; this will be our treasure and the means for our blessing. The humble believer does not serve their eyes or their belly, for God will fill them with delights if they serve him only.

> *Take delight in the Lord, and he will give you the desires of your heart.* (Ps. 37:4)

Trust humbly

> *Therefore I tell you, do not worry about your life, what you will eat or drink; or about your body,*

what you will wear. Is not life more than food, and the body more than clothes? Look at the birds of the air; they do not sow or reap or store away in barns, and yet your heavenly Father feeds them. Are you not much more valuable than they? Can any one of you by worrying add a single hour to your life?

'And why do you worry about clothes? See how the flowers of the field grow. They do not labour or spin. Yet I tell you that not even Solomon in all his splendour was dressed like one of these. If that is how God clothes the grass of the field, which is here today and tomorrow is thrown into the fire, will he not much more clothe you – you of little faith? So do not worry, saying, "What shall we eat?" or "What shall we drink?" or "What shall we wear?" For the pagans run after all these things, and your heavenly Father knows that you need them. But seek first his kingdom and his righteousness, and all these things will be given to you as well. Therefore do not worry about tomorrow, for tomorrow will worry about itself. Each day has enough trouble of its own.

I read once that 'worry is a sin' and I wondered if this was accurate. Upon reflection, even though we are all prone to worry, though in varying degrees at different times, and there's a huge variance between people (some naturally worry more than others), if we are to define sin as disobedience to God, then this command is clear. I may have concluded the last section by saying this, but Jesus states categorically that we are not to worry about anything. Not our clothing, not our food, not our drink, not tomorrow.

If we live by faith in God, and we believe in him, then any sort of worry about anything is a lack of trust. This is extremely difficult, with all the various problems we may face, but if we are to be in that place of surrender to him, there should be no room for such negative thoughts. I should know, and must constantly remind myself, that my needs have always been met. I may go through a period of lack in order to learn patience and to lean on him completely, but I have never starved or lost my home, and don't believe I ever will. Many will scoff at this, and say that I only 'excuse away' those times as 'lessons' in order to maintain that God is good to me. No. I know that he has always been good, and will never forsake me.

How, though, can I be able to be constantly aware of my situation as under his guiding and caring hand? Is there a way to do this? If we are busy about doing these things, these beautiful commands, then we shall be more aware of the needs of others, and get some perspective on our own plights. When we worry about those things we need for sustenance, remember to do good, for if we only *seek first his kingdom and his righteousness*, then *all these things will be given to [us] as well.*

Praise his glorious name.

Part 3: The Heart Transformed

Back to (not) Judging

> *Do not judge, or you too will be judged. For in the
> same way as you judge others, you will be judged,
> and with the measure you use, it will be measured
> to you.*
> *'Why do you look at the speck of sawdust in your
> brother's eye and pay no attention to the plank in
> your own eye? How can you say to your brother,
> "Let me take the speck out of your eye," when all
> the time there is a plank in your own eye? You
> hypocrite, first take the plank out of your own eye,
> and then you will see clearly to remove the speck
> from your brother's eye.*
> *'Do not give dogs what is sacred; do not throw
> your pearls to pigs. If you do, they may trample
> them under their feet, and turn and tear you to
> pieces.*

We go right back now to that tree! It was the original reason
for losing Eden, wasn't it? Why would Jesus not begin with
this? Surely we all tend to react against such a command to
not judge, because we all love doing it? Nothing makes us
feel better than passing a judgement on somebody else, and
patting ourselves on the back for being 'better than them'. I
have heard so many excuses, get-out clauses and
workarounds from other believers about how we have to be
able to judge others. Often the spin of 'discernment' is put
on it, and how discerning people is good and necessary. A
genuine concern is that we need to know if we can trust
somebody, don't we? It certainly is wise to know how to

deal with all people, and discerning someone as not very trustworthy, or recognising they are a known liar, will set you up in a better position to know how to deal with them. That's given. So does this command mean that we're now allowed to make such reasoned decisions? This is a tricky one, but by taking other things that Jesus said, and a seasoning from Paul's teaching, we can arrive at a good place.

Jesus did give us a savvy lesson with *I am sending you out like sheep among wolves. Therefore be as shrewd as snakes and as innocent as doves* (Matt. 10:16). The context of this, as he states, is when he was sending out the twelve with the gospel message. The warning following this was about being persecuted in the town councils and synagogues, and how they were not to fear but trust that they would find the words easily by the leading of the Spirit. I do think we can apply this principle here. Snakes were seen as clever and wily hunters who could creep up on prey silently, so his analogy applied would mean that in our dealings with others, we must be aware and alert. However, we are also to be as 'innocent as doves', so how do we balance this? Many people have an avid aversion to snakes; they aren't the most beautiful of God's creatures, and we know a lot of them can kill us with a bite or by constriction, whereas I've never heard of anyone who fears doves or thinks they're ugly. Therefore we must present to others as beautifully and as innocently as we would imagine a dove to be, while within we are being shrewd. Does this mean we are making judgements about others? I would say that we make decisions on their actions, and what they might do to us or not, but that does not mean we are judging their motives or their character.

Let me clarify from another incident in this gospel, which is a well-known passage; after Peter has made the confession that Jesus is '*the Messiah, the Son of the living God*' (16:16), he then tries to tell his master that the very idea of him going to Jerusalem to suffer and be killed is not acceptable and that he will stop this. Jesus turns on him in an instant and rebukes him:

> *Jesus turned and said to Peter, 'Get behind me, Satan! You are a stumbling-block to me; you do not have in mind the concerns of God, but merely human concerns.'* (Matt. 16:23)

Laying aside the problem that Peter had in accepting how his death was instrumental to Jesus' mission, why is Jesus calling him 'Satan'? I think we are missing something in this incident that would have been apparent to the twelve present at that time. Having studied linguistics and communication, it is obvious to me and my academic colleagues that the different means of communication contain many aspects that are unique to that particular means. I find it very difficult to give emphasis and weight to some words more than others while writing this, which I hope I can maintain in formatting when it comes to making this available electronically. This is not a problem when speaking, since we use differences in volume and intonation, combined with non-verbal gestures and facial expressions. I'm going to state that I don't believe Jesus was calling Peter Satan! That would be a personal insult, and would be so out of character with our Lord. Why would he have preached about not saying things like 'Raca' to someone, and then be guilty of it himself?

One of my most heartfelt blogs was when I thought about how Jesus addressed people; was he really nasty and insulting? I knew that he had called the Pharisees things like 'a brood of vipers', 'whitewashed tombs' and 'the blind leading the blind', so I sat down and did a speed read of the four gospels, noting all the words that Jesus uttered. NOWHERE does he insult an individual, except for this one glaring exception! All the times he was disparaging towards people, it was directed at a group. This scenario where he rebukes Peter being the single exception, my question was then 'why?' I don't believe I was able to answer that when I wrote the blog, but on reflection, I realised what Jesus was actually saying. Think of the emphasis here: "Get behind ME, Satan!" This is **how** he was saying it! His beloved disciple had made the confession of faith in him, and now was only making an error. A huge one, yes, that deserved to be addressed, but Jesus would have known he only lacked the comprehension.

There is much debate in theology about Satan/ the Satan/ Lucifer, and who he is, or if he is an actual individual, or a spirit of evil, or the evil that exists within us all. I personally believe in the existence of this fallen angel because I believe Jesus stated it, but I cannot believe he is omnipresent (everywhere at once, like God), so how can he be behind every evil thing that happens to me and to you? The word satan from the Hebrew means 'accuser' and can be found with the article to mean 'the accuser'. It can also mean in some contexts, 'opposer'. However, the Greek record here is clearly the capitalised name. Jesus is addressing an entity, but is he addressing Peter?

When we think of how Satan (or evil entities) attack us, we should be mindful of Paul's allegory. To the Ephesians, he warned them *take up the shield of faith, with which you can extinguish all the flaming arrows of the evil one* (6:16). How often do we make statements like 'the Devil is using that person to get at you/me' or 'he doesn't realise that he's doing the Devil's work'? If we think of how the opposite of courage is cowardice, then we should well expect this from the Father of Lies. He loves to find others to manipulate, through poor understanding, lack of spiritual maturity/ courage, or plain fear, to do what he wants them to do. He *prowls around like a roaring lion looking for someone to devour* (1Pet. 5:8), and once he finds that someone, he makes them an unwitting agent in his plans. I form the picture in my mind of a cowardly archer, hiding behind a human shield while firing the arrows at me. Once I have this picture, then the person who is opposing or attacking me, maybe even accusing me of certain things which are untrue, is only an instrument in the hands of evil, and not actually inherently evil themselves. If you have the belief in 'total depravity' then you may find this hard to swallow. It's an aspect of Calvinistic thought that I have rejected as a poor interpretation of scripture along with the Augustinian definition of 'original sin' that we discussed. We could enter into a huge debate about the nature of evil; for example, we could agree that Adolf Hitler was an evil person, but was the young boy Adolf evil, or did circumstances make him become evil? If we have a starting point that every human is born evil, then there's little we can do really, in my opinion, but the fatalism of Calvin would always make anything we do pointless since it's all pre-ordained anyway. I'm leaving that for a totally separate work that I might never even wish to write! What I do with these teachings I wrestle with is more important to me; **how** I deal with those who attack me, and act against me.

We all make choices. We do this when we meet someone, when we first engage them in conversation, and after we get to know them a bit better. We can choose to see the good things about them, or the bad, or accept that everyone is a mixture of good and bad. It's peculiar that we try to define strangers more as either/or while we are more honest about close friends and family. This is because in time we get to see all the different characteristics that make them who they are. Therefore, someone who might attack me for some reason could be forgiven more easily if I already know them well enough, and recognise the action as 'out-of-character' or for a specific reason. I'm less likely to forgive if they're a stranger, and even less if I see them as an enemy. This is where 'enemy love' comes into play; if Jesus has commanded us to love our enemies, then we should treat them in the same way we would a dear brother or sister. The choice is to not allow anything negative or any animosity to be the defining trait for them. If we are able to look behind this, and try to see just why they have behaved in such a way, would we not be able to see that lurking archer popping out to fire the arrow every now and then?

In psychological terms, people who have certain issues listed under 'mental health' usually have underlying reasons for their illness. A young parent making the effort to keep things clean to protect their baby from germs in the environment might develop an obsessiveness with cleanliness that becomes OCD. The condition might be annoying to live with, but if the reason for it can be discerned, that can help to comprehend and even treat it. Likewise, someone who expresses anger and hostility might well have an original good reason for it, and can be helped to deal with their anger once recognised. I had an issue as an 'angry young man' that was discovered and dealt with many years ago - there was a genuine reason for it, but it was destroying me from within. Now I'm a 'grumpy old git' but that's a different matter (and probably incurable!).

This is what I truly believe Jesus was saying when he addressed Peter. He saw the work of Satan **behind** Peter, and rebuked the influence upon Peter's thinking. Yes, he was rebuking Peter, but the accusation of 'Satan!' was to address the cause, and he was daring Satan to get out from behind Peter and told him to 'get behind ME!' where he would be able to deal with him by ignoring him or refuting him, just as he did in the wilderness. Satan would know not to tempt him anymore after that experience! We should send Satan to Jesus when we hear him tempting us with unholy words, since he can deal with him like he has always done.

Just as you're reacting against this, in the most natural way, protesting that you won't be able to do that when you see hostility come your way, and can only perceive it as a force of evil against you, there's a help offered. That plank in your own eye has to come out! Jesus makes the great point that none of us have clean eyes, or are without sin, as he showed so expertly in assuaging the anger of he crowd with 'the woman caught in adultery' (John 8:1-11). I loved a blog by Brian Zahnd where he explained how Jesus not only saved the woman, but saved the angry crowd from their own wrath, and stopped them from killing. Jesus actually makes the point that what we see in someone else's eye is only a speck of sawdust compared to the huge plank in ours! How can we try to say that 'our' sin or problem is nothing compared to that other person's, once we've been delivered this stinger? We know that sometimes that sawdust in the other person's eye truly is worse than ours, but Jesus is giving us the instructions on what to do when following him; note that he calls us a hypocrite if we don't **first** remove our own plank so that we will be **able** to see the sawdust clearly. In other words, we cannot start trying to help others remove specks until our own vision is clear, and that means recognising our own faults.

When I did a basic evening course in counselling, we were told that the first step to counselling was to know ourselves. We had to analyse personality tests on our own character, and grasp how we react to things, how we process thoughts, and how we interact with others, **before** we could ever start helping others. Once you become aware of your own foibles, you are much less likely to bounce all over someone else for their mistakes. This doesn't mean that you become perfect and never give in to your faults, or can avoid your triggers without ever reacting, but it truly is key to reaching that place where you become averse to making judgements on others. Again, you'll always be prone to it, but it diminishes the more self-aware you are.

So a major key to put into the lock of this door is: humility. Everything that was covered in part 2 now becomes practical. The heart change that Jesus called us to seek in part 1 is honoured and assisted by the application of simple subservience to your calling to follow the Servant King and to serve as he showed us. The honest sense that you are not really any better than anybody else is what oils the mechanism and releases the cogs of the lock so you can enter into true and worthwhile fellowship with those around you.

> *For by the grace given me I say to every one of you: do not think of yourself more highly than you ought, but rather think of yourself with sober judgment, in accordance with the faith God has distributed to each of you.* (Romans 12:3)

Taking this statement from Paul in its context, we should note that in the preceding verse, he exhorts us: *Do not conform to the pattern of this world, but be transformed by the renewing of your mind.* So one of the first instructions given by Paul when addressing 'worldliness' is this seeking of humility, and it is what should happen when we 'renew' our mind and our thinking. Paul gets it, and very often he tries to instruct his readers on the nature of this perfect love and the way to follow once we embark on it.

Please note, however, that just as you are to behave as one not any better than another, you are also, conversely, not any worse than another. Recall my disdain for false humility. What is often found alongside that is what some call 'worm theology', which is a denigration of oneself to the point that one thinks they are of no worth or cannot be valued in any way. While it is humility that keeps us from becoming conceited, we should not allow it to make us shamefaced and fearful. Did Jesus not come to this earth for you and me? Did he not give his life for you and me? Are we not children of the Most High God? True humility recognises our place in the universe, neither too highly nor too lowly.

> *"Humility is not thinking less of yourself, it's thinking of yourself less."*
>
> - CS Lewis

Right after this, we come across an oft-quoted verse, very often used out of context: *Do not give dogs what is sacred; do not throw your pearls to pigs. If you do, they may trample them under their feet, and turn and tear you to pieces.* Why would it sit here in this context? Why talk about pearls and pigs? Is what we have just read and analysed not a pearl of wisdom? So is this the very sort of pearl that we should not 'throw to pigs'? I anticipate some reaction against what I have said, and I will be very, very pleasantly surprised if it draws no criticism from those who really have no desire to engage with it, therefore I will probably get 'torn to pieces' for it. Should that make me not publish this? Should I only provide this book for those who are willing to listen? No! If I get vitriol for this, I trust that God will defend me for only disseminating what he taught. I will forgive such people anyway, since I am aware of how some are indoctrinated into a theology or religious system that has no place for radical ideas like those Jesus promoted. If we are asking why Jesus used 'dogs' and 'pigs'... I think if he were around today, he would probably say 'trolls'. If we distribute our Christ-inspired thoughts to the world, especially in the modern world of the internet, we must expect these 'dogs' to tear at us a bit. We **were** warned! I come across a lot of this backlash once Jesus' words are expressed, but sadly almost always from believers, not the non-believer!

Ask, seek, knock

Towards the end of this magnificent sermon which covers giving, prayer, fasting, priorities, worry, and judging, he says:

> *Ask and it will be given to you; seek and you will find; knock and the door will be opened to you. For everyone who asks receives; the one who seeks finds; and to the one who knocks, the door will be opened.*
> *Which of you, if your son asks for bread, will give him a stone? Or if he asks for a fish, will give him a snake? If you, then, though you are evil, know how to give good gifts to your children, how much more will your Father in heaven give good gifts to those who ask him!So in everything, do to others what you would have them do to you, for this sums up the Law and the Prophets.*

Oh what fantastically uplifting words! Whatever we want!? Yeah!!

This glorious passage is just one that has been taken out of context and misused and abused by those who seek to make the gospel about things other than following Jesus. When we place it in context, we see it is at the end of this long list of instructions that are about difficult concepts and practices that he wants us to follow and obey. Surely, while he was preaching these things, his audience must have been asking themselves, just as his disciples asked about that impossible camel, 'how can we do these things?' They must have recognised that his commands are near-impossible to maintain! Then he delivers his answer: ask, seek and knock! Ask for what you need and it **will** be given to you. Seek these things and you **will** find them. Knock on the door you wish to go through that you think is closed and locked to you, and… it **will** be opened to you! Who do we ask?

He provides the perfect example of a comparison between us and our Father in heaven; if we would give anything good to our children that they ask from us, because we love them even in our flawed and 'evil' ways, then **how much more** will our perfect heavenly Father give us what we ask! Note that firstly, clearly, there is **nothing** in this sermon about seeking material things or wealth! Have we not already seen that anything that Jesus has to say about material things are commanding and admonishing us to **not** go after such things, and to give money away. Now, we can safely take from this example he gave us that we will **not** receive any bad thing, since a good parent will not only avoid giving something harmful, but will also not just give a child anything they ask for, but only that which is beneficial. So we have here a promise that if we **ask** our Father for such good things, **seek** to be better followers, and **knock** on the door of achievement in living for Jesus and by his commands, we **will** be given them. The context tells us that it is things we need for his kingdom i.e. the strength and ability to do what he wants us to do. All we need to do is believe in him for achieving these Herculean tasks.

Does this mean that we will never have any good material thing? No, I don't believe that, but I do believe that we can learn to be content when we don't get the things we may want. Can you recall when you really wanted something as a child, and your parents said no to you? Maybe they couldn't afford it, or they were keen not to spoil you by giving in to every demand (I hope they **did** say no at times). I have seen my Lord supply things to me I never even expected, so I know that he will reward me with good things. Therefore, I don't need to keep pleading for them. I leave the concerns in his hands, and trust that he knows my heart, knows what I need compared to what I want, and is such a good father, that he will maybe hold off to teach me some patience and strengthen my resolve. When Paul tells me to *pray continually* (1Thess. 5:17), I don't believe that's for me, but for other people that I wish to intercede for. I know that others pray for me, and I have felt the strength of those prayers when I was in a foreign land and facing a dark experience. They did pray for me continually, as I should pray for them continually, but if I keep asking my good father for the same thing for myself over and over again, is that not a lack of trust in him, and in his nature? That's how I feel about it, but as they say, your mileage may vary.

I will repeat, though, that the context dictates to us that these promises are all to do with empowering us for achieving his kingdom on earth, and to become the powerful and effective witnesses of his nature and his gospel to the world. It **can** be done. If you want to try to define what the *good gifts* are that he refers to, note that in Luke's account of Jesus saying this, that is replaced by *the Holy Spirit*. Therefore these are good **spiritual** things! In essence, we will not and **cannot** do this on our own, and this is where the licensers fall down. They look at 'standards' within scripture, and determine that it's just too difficult, so choose to walk away from any effort. However, if we know that we are saved by grace and not works (Eph. 2:8,9) and must not think that any effort we make will save us, then we can rest in contentment at our position with Christ in being already ransomed from the consequences of sin, but that same 'lack of effort' must also translate into understanding that indeed we are **not** to rely on our own efforts and strength for our walk, but on **his** strength, just as our salvation is rested upon him. It's not just our salvation, our justification, but also this process that is called sanctification which rests on him! Praise his name! Another well-known verse from the pen of Paul: *I can do all this through him who gives me strength* (Phil. 4:13) is a great one to remember. However, keep in mind yet again, the context: Paul wrote this letter from prison! The preceding verse of these closing remarks, from his locked cell… *I know what it is to be in need, and I know what it is to have plenty. I have learned the secret of being content in any and every situation, whether well fed or hungry, whether living in plenty or in want.*

In my following of Jesus, I have always been certain, right from the day I was awestruck by seeing his beautiful example, that following him means trying to be **like** him. I do not use the word 'implies' or 'suggests' or even that I **think** or 'have a belief' about it. I **know**, for sure, that if I am a follower of his, a true disciple, then my aim in life is to obey him and seek to be more like him, to the best of my ability. It is **not** just another religious dogma to adhere to, or a doctrine to believe in, let alone a church to attend or a denomination to belong to. It **is**, first and foremost, a path to follow, a person to believe in and someone to give my life to. He is the way, the truth and the life (John 14:6), and so he should be **my** way, **my** truth, and **my** life. The early church even called this path that they were on 'The Way'! Let us follow it, but seek out his footsteps in which to place our feet, not in our own understanding or strength, but in his. In relying upon him, shall we surely not find the strength that does not reside in our own fallen selves? To finish this section, this is where Jesus states that we must *do to others what you would have them do to you* and so he is exhorting us to do good works to others (not passively doing no evil, but **actively** doing good), since *this sums up the Law and the Prophets*. Salvation is not achieved by good works, but good works must follow salvation.

> *"By the law was the knowledge of sin, but by the gospel was the conquest of it."*
>
> - Matthew Henry

The Narrow Way

> *Enter through the narrow gate. For wide is the gate and broad is the road that leads to destruction, and many enter through it. But small is the gate and narrow the road that leads to life, and only a few find it.*

Some passages can give us many messages. I have heard great preachers expound a piece of scripture for the nth time in their career, yet they have found a jewel within it that they had not proclaimed before. This is one passage that I have always thought I understood. Many will easily find the broad and smooth path that does not lead to life and will follow it unknowingly. Not so many will find the true path to life. However, is this all that we have to glean from this? As I have just testified to my desire to follow Jesus myself on The Way that I found as the lone 14-year old atheist at that Christian camp, so I have revisited that experience in my later years: I concluded that if I was able to follow, and grow all on my own for the first period, I could do it again. I have no desire to leave fellowship behind me. In fact, I will crave true and good fellowship for the rest of my life. I think the thoughts came when I was seriously considering moving to France and discovering that some rural areas have no church within around 90 miles! Could we do the move and continue in our faith? Of course we could; fellowship is very important and extremely valuable, but not vital. We each come to Christ on our own, so that is an individual decision to follow too.

[I am planning to discuss church, fellowship and community in my next book]

Armed with this recollection that I certainly did live and grow without fellowship at the start, I was struck with a new view of the 'narrow gate'. I have consistently been aware of how thinking can be shaped by society around us, and we sometimes don't even perceive it. Advertisers and politicians alike seek to profile you for your needs and desires, and to target you with what **they** want to sell you or convince you. Very sadly, many church leaders (I shall not call them pastors) also adopt such tactics to control people! Following the crowd, or the flock, is the clearest example of 'worldly thinking'. While many preachers proclaim that they won't go along with the worldly view of infidelity and the denigration of marriage, which I totally concur with, they too often tend to 'go with the flow' on many other issues, just because it has become the 'standard practice' or 'orthodox interpretation' of their peers. This is all too easy, frankly. Stand on a few hot button topics that really don't affect you and ignore the more difficult ones. Though very many of those who shout about family values have been found playing away from home, or worse!

If we want to examine what worldliness is about, we should repeat this lesson from Paul (probably my favourite single verse): *Do not conform to the pattern of this world, but be transformed by the renewing of your mind. Then you will be able to test and approve what God's will is – his good, pleasing and perfect will* (Rom. 12:2). He calls to each of us, as individuals, to break free from the groupthink, and be free to hear his own Spirit and voice within ourselves. Thus I came to see the narrow gate as the one that I alone walked through to find Jesus. I am sure that your gate was different to mine, though maybe similar in some ways, since all gates have a basic construction. I imagine each would have a different lock, different materials, colour, height, weight. Some are easier to open than others. Some have been rusted and bound and need freeing.

There was a forest I used to walk through near where I lived. The gravel path ran around it in the prescribed way, but I once noticed a little clearing between the trees where a dark track was apparent. I decided to follow it, for the peace of the seclusion of the trees. I found a small clearing where there was a fallen trunk to sit on and meditate. Nobody else came that way, ever.

Two roads diverged in a wood, and I—
I took the one less traveled by,
And that has made all the difference.

- Robert Frost

If you can see the gate as your own, then you are one of those who has opened the gate, gone through, and embarked upon this way. Along this narrow path, we will all accompany each other, rest together, rest alone, take our own pace, meet up again... what a journey it has been, and will still be! Follow your heart, for if Christ is truly residing there, it will resonate with his voice.

True and False

... prophets

Watch out for false prophets. They come to you in sheep's clothing, but inwardly they are ferocious wolves. By their fruit you will recognise them. Do people pick grapes from thorn-bushes, or figs from thistles? Likewise, every good tree bears good fruit, but a bad tree bears bad fruit. A good tree cannot bear bad fruit, and a bad tree cannot bear good fruit. Every tree that does not bear good fruit is cut down and thrown into the fire. Thus, by their fruit you will recognise them.

Now we come back to discerning between good and bad, authentic and fake, true and false. While we are commanded to avoid judging, there are tools available to us to allow us to take on that snake-like mantle. I still believe that in all our dealings with people being discerned here, honesty, dove-like peace and above all, love, should be displayed. This is the rule for 'false prophets' i.e. those who are in leadership and those who would seek to teach and instruct, or tell us that they know the way of God and can show us. By writing this very book, I put myself up to be examined as a prophet, since I am daring to expound the words of Christ. That is the ministry of a prophet (not the gift); to give God's words to the people, to explain them, and to make them clear and effective. If you have grasped how you walk your own path, and are able to hear that Spirit within you speak, then you can decide for yourself whether what I say (or anybody says) resonates with that or not. While there are many that have gone before me with wisdom and experience, and I have valued their input, I must, at the end of the day, make my own decisions. I have been told on more than one occasion, to 'not go near that church' or to avoid 'reading anything by this writer'. Had I heeded such instructions, I would never have moved forward in my walk, or found blessing in corners I had not expected. I have to trust the guiding hand of God on my own life, and not the things that guided someone else. If what they tell me does actually match up with my path, then I take that on board, but I discern each and every thing, and I should also discern each and every person. This is the instruction here; examine the fruit that a self-proclaimed prophet produces. Note that they come *in sheep's clothing* i.e. they will **look** right, and innocent. How many people are chosen for leadership because they dress well, or even if they look attractive, or they have an air of charm and confidence about them? It's the content and the results of their ministry that is to be looked at. Some have been chosen just because they mimic an older preacher in their style!

I have heard a few times: God doesn't want me to judge, but he does want me to be a fruit inspector! Exactly! We are not judging a person or their nature, their background, their soul, their salvation, but we **are** looking at those who are trying to lead us, and asking ourselves what fruit they produce. If it's not good fruit that you wish to eat, why choose to bask under the shade of their branches? If no good fruit is present, we will eventually starve, surely? The transformed heart that is heeding these words of Christ, and walking its own path confidently in the right direction, will be able to see each tree along the way with clearer vision, and spend time beneath the ones that provide good fruit. The trees that don't will serve no purpose so don't hang around waiting for an apple to fall when there's nothing there, or nothing that isn't sour or inedible! If you are able to get sustenance from those good trees by your own discernment, then the barren trees will not trouble you as much, though I would say that if you are able, you should help others to find the good fruit, and even take it to them yourself, to redirect them away from the bad trees.

... followers

'Not everyone who says to me, "Lord, Lord," will enter the kingdom of heaven, but only the one who does the will of my Father who is in heaven. Many will say to me on that day, "Lord, Lord, did we not prophesy in your name and in your name drive out demons and in your name perform many miracles?" Then I will tell them plainly, "I never knew you. Away from me, you evildoers!"

So we have decided to take Jesus' advice on prophets and spiritual leaders, but that doesn't apply to the rest of us, the laity? I actually don't like to emphasise distinctions between 'laity' and 'leadership' since we are all priests now (1Pet. 2:9; Rev. 5:10), but I have always been very careful to not make a judgement upon an individual's salvation or standing with God. That is entirely up to him, and not us at all. Those who make declarations on that towards others are in danger of being 'under judgement', I believe. I cite Jimmy Swaggart as evidence in that case.

Therefore, we are not in a position to decide about others, but what about ourselves? I have known people who have terrible trouble accepting the grace that has been extended to them, and worry day and night if they **are** 'saved' or a true believer. We have examined how there is something utterly scandalous about the gospel of grace, and how it is extended to all, and now we are brought right back to this question; how can we be assured? A simple childlike acceptance of it is required, and that should be the end of it. However, some of us are deep thinkers and wrestle with these things too much. I personally have never struggled with this, and I really wish I could give others the same deep assurance that I have. It is more precious than anything; truly a 'great pearl'. Once you discover it, you will forsake everything else to have and keep it (Matt. 13:45-6).

I think that, sadly, the modern church has placed too much emphasis on belief, in the wake of the rejection of 'salvation by works', and thus 'correct doctrine' is the determiner for many on standing with God. When I think about it, I can't imagine God judging me at the great seat on the great day, saying "No, you didn't believe in 'soul sleep' and you never really fully accepted penal substitutionary atonement. Away from me!" These are the various labels and criteria that we put upon faith. I love theology, and love debating it, but there has to be a better means of establishing who is 'in' and who is 'out'. I can reject the doctrine of a church or denomination, or parts of it, and have no desire to join their congregation, but still find genuine believers within their walls. I believe God judges each of us based on what **we** accept and believe, and not what is preached from the pulpit we sit under. Pastors and teachers are set for a different and stricter reckoning with God (James 3:1).

If it is only correct doctrine, then it is those who proclaim Jesus as their saviour and nothing else. This is often what we are told, is it not? Those who say 'Lord, Lord,' - that's what that is saying. We have to be careful that in our enthusiasm to preach the scandal of grace, we do not overreach our own Lord and make trivial or worthless something that Jesus holds as important. He clearly tells us that it is **not** everyone who says 'Lord, Lord.' who will enter his kingdom; *only the one who does the will of my Father who is in heaven* is the one he accepts. So is this actually 'salvation by works'? Some denominations will take this to be the case, and thus they also fall into error, in trying to make their congregants pursue after salvation and acceptance, and burden them with a lifetime of just never knowing if 'they have done enough' or have been 'good enough' to avoid destruction. What a religious life of trauma would that be? I have no idea of that burden. None at all. I can only imagine. Once I rest in Jesus, and know that his love is complete, and he has achieved everything, I can simply accept it.

So what exactly is Jesus saying here? He tells us that there will be some who come claiming that they know him as Lord, and even how they prophesied, exorcised demons and performed miracles! In his name!! He will say he never knew them. Therefore, these actions, which many in the church take to be what the church is called to do, are **not** doing *the will of my Father*. What is the Father's will is all that we have examined so far, all that Jesus has just taught his followers. This is what marks you out as 'one of his'. We have also, I hope, seen how these things are achieved, by the asking and seeking for his help and strength to do them. His grace will provide for us. Therefore the one who has managed to transform their heart to be leaning towards Jesus will be the one who will do these things, because a desire has been borne within their chest to do so. We all know that the best result of parenting is a child who wishes to please us by doing what we want them to do out of love for us and a natural desire to make us happy, and not just because we said so, or to avoid a punishment. The child who does not obey a good parent will face a punishment as a consequence, but the good parent will win them over to be a better child, thus a better adult, a better person. Happiness is knowing that you raised good kids. Our Father in heaven is happy when he knows he has raised us to be the one who does his will, because he has made our hearts better, and mended any scars that might exist in them from past experiences. The one who displays that they have no desire to follow these commands simply show that their heart is unchanged and have never truly experienced the transforming power of the love of Jesus.

*If I speak with human eloquence and angelic
ecstasy but don't love, I'm nothing but the creaking
of a rusty gate.
If I speak God's Word with power, revealing all his
mysteries and making everything plain as day, and
if I have faith that says to a mountain, "Jump," and
it jumps, but I don't love, I'm nothing.
If I give everything I own to the poor and even go
to the stake to be burned as a martyr, but I don't
love, I've gotten nowhere. So, no matter what I say,
what I believe, and what I do, I'm bankrupt without
love.* (1Cor.13:1-7 MSG)

I do not hold to the Calvinist doctrine of 'irresistible grace'
but I certainly do believe in the 'indefatigable love' of
Jesus. If it shines upon your heart, you **will** be transformed.
Just let the light in, and do not make your eye evil towards
it, or you will remain in darkness within. Let him (in the
words of Bono) 'kick the darkness till it bleeds daylight'.
Otherwise you will end up with just a church to sit in with
nothing real within it.

*I stopped outside a church house
Where the citizens like to sit.
They say they want the kingdom
But they don't want God in it.*

- U2

Wisdom and Folly

*Therefore everyone who hears these words of mine
and puts them into practice is like a wise man who*

141

built his house on the rock. The rain came down, the streams rose, and the winds blew and beat against that house; yet it did not fall, because it had its foundation on the rock. But everyone who hears these words of mine and does not put them into practice is like a foolish man who built his house on sand. The rain came down, the streams rose, and the winds blew and beat against that house, and it fell with a great crash.'

Hear these words! Put them into practice! Your house will be built upon a solid rock. We often hear that this is a parable of Jesus that refers to himself i.e. we must build our house upon **him**, for he is the rock. Yes, he is our foundation, and our recognition of him is truly a foundation; as he said to Peter upon his confession that Jesus was the Son of the living God: *And I tell you that you are Peter, and on this rock I will build my church...* (Matt. 16:18). Somehow we miss what Jesus is telling us to **do**, to make that house firm upon the rock: hear the words he has spoken and obey them. The converse is the foolish one who did not build upon the rock. They did hear Jesus' words but didn't *put them into practice*. Just sitting in a church and hearing the words of Jesus spoken to you will not do it. If you don't act upon them and do what he says, your house will fall *with a great crash* when the storms come. You will not survive the onslaught of the world and the Devil, and all that they throw at you.

Like me, you may wonder just how these things can be put into practice, and how doing them will solve many problems for us. A situation occurred in my life where I had to actually do this, against everything that was natural to me. I had fallen out with someone in my life some years before. I was thinking that maybe it was time to 'bury the hatchet' and heal the rift for the sake of those dear to me. However, I knew that I wasn't ready to trust this person. My perception of them was that they would use this chance to begin their controlling techniques again, and cause havoc just like they did before. I recalled all these commands about loving my enemy, and turning the other cheek. Was I to be ready to actually turn my other cheek to them after they had slapped it before? Would they do it again? Would I be willing to turn it yet again? I wrestled with what was being said to me in my heart.

In the famous chapter on love, 1 Corinthians 13, Paul says that love *always trusts* (v.7). If this is meant to be the inspired word of God that I'm reading, how can this be true? **Always** trusts? If I know that someone is **not** trustworthy, then am I not discerning this for a reason? As I pondered this, I recognised that if love trusts, then complete love trusts completely, and perfect love trusts perfectly. The love of Christ is perfect, therefore it is worthy of being trusted perfectly and completely. Faith allows me to apply this, so I decided to follow the inner voice and do as my heart asked me to do, while trusting God completely to work things out for me. I wrote a letter to this person, and sent it in faith, having left it with God in prayer.

The reaction to it was not what I expected, at all. Even though it was conciliatory, and humble, it provoked this person to fury, and they turned on me in a way that showed a few others exactly who was in the wrong, once they had seen what I wrote, and not what they were told I had written. I wondered how this could have happened;

143

Do not take revenge, my dear friends, but leave
room for God's wrath, for it is written: 'It is mine
to avenge; I will repay,' says the Lord. On the
contrary:
'If your enemy is hungry, feed him;
*   if he is thirsty, give him something to drink.*
In doing this, you will heap burning coals on his
head.'
Do not be overcome by evil, but overcome evil with
good. (Rom. 12:19-21)

Paul reiterates what is written in Deuteronomy and the
Psalms to repeat what Jesus taught. Doing 'the right thing'
to an enemy **will** heap burning coals on their head. Then the
choice is up to them to shake them off and respond, or just
let them burn. If they are too dumb or too blind to be able
to shake off the coals, that becomes their problem.

The consequence was that this person had the chance to be
reconciled with me, and my children, but lost it. I had
nothing more to do. Had they accepted the offer of my
olive branch, that would have been a win/win, but that was
out of my hands. I believe the result was the best outcome
that God wanted for me. If we simply obey what Jesus has
said, without any reservations about what the outcome
might be, or what others might think, then I believe we will
be honoured for being obedient servants. If I had not
obeyed my Lord, I would have been foolish, and a lot of
this might have come down with a great crash. Practice
makes perfect, they say. With Jesus, practice of his words
creates the perfect result.

The Verdict

> *When Jesus had finished saying these things, the crowds were amazed at his teaching, because he taught as one who had authority, and not as their teachers of the law.*

Just in case anyone is at the place of thinking that they can dismiss or get around these words in some way, remember that the hearers knew that Jesus spoke **with authority** and not as any teacher of the law. You may reject some of the things I have said here, since I am fallible, and I recognise that some of this is just my opinion. I hope I have been able to distinguish between my opinion and the literal words of Jesus. Often it is not easy, because we are all on our own path and we all listen to our own heart. I simply exhort you to make every effort to allow your heart to change its tune to be more like what Jesus wants, and not what you think he wants. A lot of his teaching is counter-intuitive and frankly, weird, in this world. When people tell me that I'm weird, I say 'thank you' because I never want to be like the crowd, the world, the other teachers that only parrot what other teachers told them. Get back to the master and what he said, and if you find things that I have missed, you will have been blessed. I hope you can share that with others for their benefit.

My real wish is for you who have come to know Jesus, to know him better. Open the door and invite him in for something to eat with you, and just listen.

Grace be with you.

Printed in Poland
by Amazon Fulfillment
Poland Sp. z o.o., Wrocław

59505864R00094